DIFFERENT ENCLOSURES

by Irena Klepfisz

ONLYWOMEN PRESS

Published by Onlywomen Press Ltd., 38 Mount Pleasant, London WC1 (1985)

ISBN 0 906500 17 6

Printed in Great Britain by Redwood Burn Ltd., Trowbridge, Wiltshire.

Cover design Pat Schaverien.

periods of stress was first published by Out & Out Books, New York, 1975.
they're always curious first appeared in HERESIES 3, 1977.
The Journal of Rachel Robotnik first appeared in CONDITIONS : SIX, New York, 1980.
Keeper of Accounts was first published by Persephone Press, Inc., Watertown, Mass., U.S.A., 1982. All distribution now through *Sinister Wisdom*, Rockland, Me., U.S.A.

ABOUT THE AUTHOR

Irena Klepfisz was born in Warsaw, Poland in 1941. She emigrated to the United States in 1949 and grew up in New York City. A graduate of the City College of New York she received her Ph.D. in English from the University of Chicago. She has taught English, Yiddish, Women's Studies, and women's poetry workshops and has supported herself primarily as a secretary, copyeditor, proofreader, typist and word processor. In 1975 she received a New York State CAPS grant in poetry. She was a founding editor of *Conditions* magazine (1976 — 1981). Her fiction, poetry and essays have appeared in Jewish, feminist and lesbian/feminist magazines. A Jewish lesbian/ feminist activist, she has conducted workshops and written on anti-Semitism, Jewish identity, the holocaust, issues facing the American Jewish writer, feminism and office work. Together with Melanie Kaye/Kantrowitz she is editing a special issue of *Sinister Wisdom* (No. 29/30) on Jewish women's identity.

Published work by Irena Klepfisz includes:

periods of stress, Out & Out Books, New York, U.S.A. 1975.
(Out of print.)

"Women Without Children/Women Without Families/Women Alone", *Conditions 2* (1977) and anthologised in *Why Children?*, Women's Press, London, 1980.

"Anti-Semitism in the Lesbian/Feminist Movement", Womanews, New York, 1981 and anthologised in *Nice Jewish Girls; a lesbian anthology*, Persephone Press, Massachusetts, U.S.A. 1982, available from The Crossing Press, Trumansburg, New York, U.S.A.

"Resisting and Surviving America", anthologised in *Nice Jewish Girls; a lesbian anthology,* 1982.

Keeper of Accounts, Persephone Press, Massachusetts, U.S.A. 1982. All distribution now through *Sinister Wisdom,* Rockland, Me., U.S.A.

"The Distances Between Us: Feminism, Sisterhood and the Girls at the Office", *Sinister Wisdom* No. 28, 1985.

CONTENTS

periods of stress

Keeper of Accounts

periods of stress

I

during the war
germans were known
to pick up infants
by their feet
swing them through the air
and smash their heads
against plaster walls.

somehow
i managed
to escape that fate.

p o w's

the p o w's   came   home   some after
seven years   a long time   to return to
a wife   suddenly reaching   her menopause
a daughter   menstruating   every month
it's a hard lesson   to understand:
wrinkled thighs   and sagging breasts

my father came home   to me   for the first time
in twenty-nine years   just last night   in a
dream   he was old   and tired
and so scarred   so very unlike   the image
i have of him   he pulled his hat   down
over his eyes   ashamed   of his years   his shabbiness
and waited   on the staircase   hoping   i'd say
welcome home   dad
                         he was thirty   killed
by a german   machine gun   defending   the roof
of a brush factory   was declared   a hero
awarded   the highest medal   a soldier could
get awarded   posthumously
                         i am now   almost thirty-
two   should have borne   him a grandson   to carry
his name   he came home   a bit   early

11

herr captain

i whispered as he came   through the gate
captain   i am clean   i've been trained
well   i said   captain   i'm not over
used

he was hard   so hard   forcing bending me
till i could not breathe   slamming against me
my mouth filled with terror   i was pierced
in two   when he suddenly pulled out
my head back   he murmured   what a light rider
my grandmother   too   rode her cossack lover
in pain he moaned   harder quicker   ride me now
fearful i ran   jumping the gate   with the guards
laughing   grimacing   through the window   nervous
biting their nails   the dogs barked   my legs spread   slapped
around his waist   i whipped him further   deeper   till
i felt the blood flooding the field   filling the drowning well
lapping over me   drinking in the smell of his hair
his stomach swollen against me   he collapsed
but i held on   pushing my heels into his back
my teeth clenched   i hissed for my grandmother   her crooked wig
her gold teeth   and her cossack lover   crawling from the well she
pushed up her buttocks   as she came over the wall   fell to the ground
head   first her wig cocked over one eye a butcher knife under her
skirt my mother floats in well water zeyde in mourning tears his red
hair hears them again on the kitchen floor slipping in so smoothly she
was wet from the beginning the horse neighing outside and bobe her ear
pierced at the age of three weeks pulls out the butcher knife begins
slashing till his hands severed he falls back

he brings me soap
his boots are shiny
not like the others   who arrive from the fields
crusted over

In my early teens I read *House of Dolls* (New York: Simon & Schuster, 1955),
a novel written by a man under the pseudonym Katzetnik 135633 and based on
a diary of an anonymous Jewish woman who did not survive the Holocaust.
When I rediscovered it recently, I immediately recognized it as the main uncon-
scious source for "herr captain." Although in 1984, I see sexuality and violence
from a different perspective than I did in the early 1970's when I wrote it, "herr
captain" is to me still an important poem about Jewish women's experience and
survival. — Irena Klepfisz, October 1984.

death camp

when they took us   to the shower   i saw
the rebitsin   her sagging breasts   sparse
pubic hairs   i knew   and remembered
the old rebe   and turned   my eyes away
i could still hear   her advice   a woman
with a husband   a scholar

when they turned   on the gas   i smelled
it   first   coming at me   pressed myself
hard to the wall   crying   rebitsin   rebitsin
i am here with you   and the advice you gave me
i screamed   into the wall   as the blood burst from
my lungs   cracking   her nails in women's flesh   i watched
her capsize   beneath me   my blood in her mouth   i screamed

when they dragged my body   into the oven   i burned
slowly at first   i could smell my own flesh   and could
hear   them grunt   with the weight of the   rebitsin
and they flung   her on top   of me   and i could smell
her hair burning   against my stomach

when i pressed through   the chimney
it was sunny   and clear   my smoke
was distinct   i rose quiet   left her
beneath

about my father

— he became a teetotaler out of his socialist convictions; during
    the war he began to drink again

— he was casual; he kept his tie in his pocket till the last minute
    before oral exams

— he left me on the street to be picked up by the nuns from the
    orphanage; he watched me from a distant doorway

— once he refused to hit me; he told my mother his hand was
    too large

— he wrote to his aunt that he hoped the baby would be a boy

— when he was a student, jews were not permitted to sit in the
    front rows of lecture halls; he made it a point to
    stand through the lectures; ultimately, jews were
    allowed to sit

— he was a discus thrower

— according to some, he got along with everyone: jews, goyim,
    children

— he was caught a couple of times by the germans; they thought
    he was a polish smuggler

— once he was put on a train for treblinka; he jumped, was shot at
    and wounded, but got back to warsaw alive

— he believed in resistance

perspectives on the second world war

i

       it is a terror
in the closet   her knees
are limp   eyes straining to see
every object glows with a
private halo   pulling down
her skirt   the trickle
of urine along her thigh and calf
she wipes it carelessly with her hand
biting her lips she fixates on
pebbles and rusty nails along
the path to the truck   it is an oblivion
seen in matter-of-fact gestures
wiping the child's nose with her fingers
she says   blow   his eyes shine   as she
feels the pressure of the doorknob   palms
wet slipping out of her grasp   she whispers
not now   not yet   we've been so careful
he's a good child   just a little more time
she pleads with them   we will not be
careless anymore   this time the knob falls
into the glare of lights   voices scream
orders she does not understand   but obeys
blow   she tells him pulling down her skirt
and wiping his nose with her fingers   later
it is still over   has been over
since the knob slipped from her hand
like the wet fish that jumped while she tried
to scale it   later after the not yet
not now   the walk nude across the yard
she glimpses the meaning of the order
allows her eyes to widen for one
moment and see the path   it is a coldness
never before felt or imagined   she clutches
her hands tearing at her thighs   wailing
to the others she tries to lean on them
to explain the mistake   the small error
nothing is irrevocable   she screams   nothing
to them trying to lean   they push her away
and her hands cup the knob   for a better hold
to keep out the light   her world is cement
stone   iron

ii

listening to conversations   over brandy
i am always amazed at their certainty
about the past   how it could have been
different   could have been   turned around
with what ease   they transport themselves
to another time/place   taking the comfort
confidence of an after dinner drink

                it would be too impolite
of me to say   my mother hid with me
for two years among ignorant peasants   who
would have turned us in   almost at once   had
they known who we were   who would have watched
with glee while we were carted off   even though
grandad had bounced me on his knees and fed me
from his own spoon   and my mother is a frightened
woman

                it would be too impolite
to say   you do not know yourselves   you do not know
others

from II

conditions

    i will take you   with me
next week   only if: you're
relaxed   and easy   and if:
you don't make   any trouble

if: you make any   and i mean   any
kind of trouble   i will leave you
here   with the two cats   a bowl
of water   and some   cookies

and i will be having   good times
without you   free without you
having nice times   not wishing
you were there   hanging on

and if: you choose to come
along   but spoil   my good times
and do not smile   and laugh
when it's appropriate

i will come   back without you
leave you there   among strangers
while i return   to the cats
and continue to feed them   regularly

and i will not acknowledge   any
postcards   telegrams   i will only say
you are out   or address unknown
or   you could be anywhere   by now

so let me repeat   and i do not make
idle threats   if: you want to stick
with me   and if: you want to go   and
want to come   with me   back and forth
smoothly   easily   you can   if: you do every
thing exactly   precisely   as i want

periods of stress

it is unwise during periods of stress
or change to formulate new theories.
case in point: when about to begin
a new love affair   without having ended
the previous one   do not maintain
that more freedom is required for the full expression
of individual personality   or that various
life styles are possible   and all kinds of interesting
situations   still need to be explored.

try instead: i am tired   tired
of the nearness   this small apartment
of the watering can and level of the window
shade.   i prefer to drift towards more spacious rooms
towards intimate restaurants and dimly lit unfamiliar
beds   new love techniques.   but
do not throw me out.   i am too
frightened to venture out alone.
let me stay till i'm secure again
somewhere else   and then leave me alone.

please don't touch me

please don't touch me
wait a moment
just wait one moment
until i'm not so cold

> the spider
> with its eyes
> into my insides
> the third eye
> warm with summer
> full of light
> now shrivelled
> atrophied
> dead to light

please don't touch me
wait a moment
just wait one moment
until i'm not so cold

> the spider
> with its eyes
> awake with me
> spread out
> behind my head
> silent still
> crawling away
> with the light

please don't touch me
wait a moment
just wait one moment
until i'm not so cold

the cracks
ceiling torn
caves of hollow
if breath is strong
silent still
motionless
breathless
airless
lightless
silent still
the balance
in control

please don't touch me
just wait a moment
just wait one moment
until i'm not so cold

dinosaurs and larger issues
for rachel

i

1. & 2.   the first two nights
she lay   diagonally across
the bed   clutching at the blankets
she refused me   room & warmth

3.   the third night
she told me   i can't handle
this   i can't handle   it
i slept   in the living room

4.   the fourth night
she said   this has to be
the last night   & moved
close to me

5.   the fifth night
she did not speak   about
it.

ii

they're never as big as i imagine
rachel informs me   whenever i enter
the reptile house   expecting cobras
to be jammed   wedged   bursting out of
into   every corner of the cage   muscles
tensing   i am always disappointed
with their slenderness   their comfort
and ease   as they relax   draping casually
over plastic trees

whales   she is earnest   should
be as big as ocean liners   instead
they swim content   in aquariums
trained to jump and leap   and it's true
they're large   but not like
they're supposed to be

rachel's eyes   narrow and widen
i do not reveal   some dinosaurs
full grown   were no bigger
than hens   that she could have
roasted   and served them
for dinner   with no fear of
leftovers

iii

in the dark   her features
are distinct   her skin white
translucent.   i see outlines
of bones.   she is crystal
my fingers   feel the thinness
of the flesh.   her mouth
is hard   demanding.   she
keeps her head turned away.
she does not look   directly
at me   except to brush away
the hair from my face   before
her tongue penetrates my mouth.
then her eyes close quickly.
i study the hand's gesture
try to give it meaning.

in the dark   her features
are strong.   she lies relaxed
ready to accept   the touch
of my tongue   ready to be cupped
sucked into me   later she says
i cannot reciprocate.

iv

no i don't enjoy this
she says   biting my hand.
her mouth   which holds
endless kisses   will never
say yes to me   just the hand
across my back   like a heavy hammer
or a quick furtive kiss
at the back of my neck
tell me   perhaps   yes.

i just don't like cunts
she says   i don't like
them   she says to me.

v

i am sorry if i've made
you unhappy   i told her
sitting   at the furthest end
of the couch
                    don't make
yourself so important
she answered   with confidence
there are larger issues
at stake.

vi

it's not the kind of person
you are   i try to explain to her
you have the power   to lift
your hand   to touch me as i pass
or to walk towards me   and hold
my face   so it's not the kind
of person   you are

vii

at night   the vestiges
of other ages   influence
us.   there are
the sucking sounds   of your mouth
with mine   the moans of an ancient language
i easily recognize   my tongue
urging you on   slowly   deep
beneath the sea   or in some secret
cave   our nails: clawed   we hold
each other   you and i
released from an unexpected
danger.   exhausted we lick
each other's wounds   inflict
new ones   sharply.   our voices
echo   through the cave
return   and clash   on hard rock.
we know our bodies   and do not mind
them/ourselves   losing all sense
of proportions   limits.   we are equal
here   you and i.

afterwards   in the fire's flames
we see   cumbersome dinosaurs
rubbing their necks.   against
each other   making small   sweet noises
tame and huge   so much larger than we dared imagine.

when the heart fails

when the heart fails   and over
fills with disappointment   rake
leaves   in the backyard;

gather them   in large green bags
stamp down   to make more room
gather more   and keep from the wind;

tie carefully with wire   to prevent
spillage   and going over the same ground;
since burning is forbidden   load up the car.

at the landfill   the gulls mill
and gawk   waiting.   this trip
will not please them.   there is nothing to eat.

it was good

for sharon

it was good:
the plant by your bed
green with sunlight
while we made love   your face
melted into marble
delicate pink   liquid
with desire   and later
walking through
haphazard streets
the sky empty
my arm through yours
the shrubbery   holding back
its spring greenness   your despondency
the cruising police   to remember
the slits in the blinds
the striped sun across
your face   the plant
the wetness of your mouth

flesh is cold

flesh is cold   and the bitch
moves too much in bed   crossing
and recrossing   unable to make
a warm spot and hold it   her skin
curls with the cold   shrivels
reduces her face to straight lines.
i wonder at the angle
of her back   solid in my face
she moves again   pretending
i am not there   till i pin her down
screaming   i am here   and you are not
here   alone

they're always curious

they're always curious about what you eat as if you were
some strange breed still unclassified by darwin & whether
you cook every night & wouldn't it be easier for you to
buy frozen dinners but i am quick to point out that my intra-
venous tubing has been taken out & they back up saying *i*
could never just cook for one person but i tell them it's
the same exactly the same as for two except half

but more they're curious about what you do when the urge
is on & if you use a coke bottle or some psychedelic dildo
or electric vibrator or just the good old finger or whole
hand & do you mannippppulllaaatttte yourself into a clit
orgasm or just kind of keep digging away at yourself & if
you mind it & when you have affairs doesn't it hurt when it's
over & it certainly must be lonely to go back to the old finger

& they always cluck over the amount of space you require
& certainly the extra bedroom seems unnecessary & i try to
explain that i like to move around & that i get antsy when
i have the urge so that it's nice to have an extra place
to go when you're lonely & after all it seems small compen-
sation for using the good old finger & they're surprised be-
cause they never thought of it that way & it does seem reason-
able come to think of it

& they kind of probe about your future & if you have a will or
why you bother to accumulate all that stuff or what you plan
to do with your old age & aren't you scared about being put
away somewhere or found on your bathroom floor dead after
your downstairs neighbor has smelled you out but then of course
you don't have the worry of who goes first though of course
you know couples live longer for they have something to live
for & i try to explain i live for myself even when in love but
it's a hard concept to explain when you feel lonely

Although this poem did not appear in *periods of stress*, it is included here because
it was written during the same time as many of the other poems in this collection.
periods of stress was self-published, so the omission was due solely to my own
"forgetfulness." — Irena Klepfisz, October 1984.

they did not build wings for them

they did not build wings for them
the unmarried aunts;   instead they
crammed them into old maids' rooms
or placed them as nannies with
the younger children;   mostly they
ate in the kitchen, but sometimes
were permitted to dine with the family
for which they were grateful and
smiled graciously as the food was passed.
they would eat slowly never filling
their plates and their hearts would
sink at the evening's end when it was
time to retreat into an upstairs corner.

but there were some who did not smile
who never wished to be grafted on
the bursting houses.   these few remained
indifferent to the family gatherings
preferring the aloneness of their small rooms
which they decorated with odd objects
found on long walks.   they collected
bird feathers and skulls unafraid to clean
them to whiteness;   stones which resembled
humped bears or the more common tiger and
wolf;   dried leaves whose brilliant colors
never faded;   pieces of wood still covered
with fresh moss and earth which retained
their moisture and continued flourishing.
these they placed by their dresser mirrors
in arrangements reminiscent of secret rites
or hung over delicate watercolors of unruly
trees whose branches were about to snap
with the wind.

it happened sometimes that among these
one would venture even further.   periodically
would be heard vague tales of a woman
withdrawn and inaccessible suddenly disappearing
one autumn night leaving her room bare
of herself.   women gossiped about a man.
but eventually word would come back
she had moved north to the ocean and lived
alone.   she was still collecting
but now her house was filled with crab
and lobster shells;   discolored claws
which looked like grinning south american
parrots trapped in fish nets decorated
the walls;   skulls of unidentifiable
creatures were arranged in geometric patterns
and soft reeds in tall green bottles
lined the window sills.   one room
in the back with totally bare walls
was a workshop.   here she sorted colored
shells and pasted them on wooden boards
in the shape of common flowers.   these she sold
without sentiment.

such a one might also disappear inland.
rumor would claim she had travelled in
men's clothing.   two years later it would
be reported she had settled in the woods
on some cleared land.   she ran a small farm
mainly for supplying herself with food
and wore strangely patched dresses and shawls
of oddly matched materials.   but aloneness
was her real distinction.   the house was neat
and the pantry full.   seascapes and pastoral
scenes hung on the walls.   the garden was
well kept and the flower beds clearly defined
by color: red   yellow   blue.   in the woods
five miles from the house she had an orchard.
here she secretly grafted and crossed varieties
creating singular fruit of shades and scents
never thought possible.   her experiments rarely
failed   and each spring she waited eagerly to see
what new forms would hang from the trees.
here the world was a passionate place and she
would visit it at night baring her breasts
to the moon.

the fish

for esther hyneman

directionless   it scavenged
never mapping   its own territory
or claiming   feeding rights.
it produced   spawning unfeelingly
generations unaware   of their origins
remaining indifferent   to them/it   all life
except   as it provided food   in dark shadows.

          there was no pattern   but
the broad cycle   and that also seemed
hidden from its consciousness   the irrevocable
past   present   future   so it was taken
by surprise   when suddenly it began to weaken
as the dryness entered its mouth   for it too
did not want to die   alone

it lies half   eaten   brown burnt
covered in part by sand   the mouth
agonized   almost accusatory
it would be inhuman   to disturb its pain
washed inland   it sinks and drowns.

from III

in between

it is always then
you notice   your lack
of brilliance   grace

feeling like a dying star
in the ram's horn
the fish's eye

that readies for a mute
explosion   noticed only
when its dark absence

startles a distracted astronomer.

the house

i

arranging it is far easier
than living it.   the books
stand ready on the shelves.

classifications by time or place
come naturally to me.   alone
finding the book important is difficult.

i've started to live here many mornings
opening my eyes vowing *this* morning
i will really begin.   objects intrude themselves:

floors need sweeping and one carton
unopened   is hidden in a closet.

ii

the telescope is still
disassembled   (at night
the skies are clear).

mirrors and lenses
lie in velvet lined cases.
i am afraid to use them.

iii

one of my cats was badly
clawed.   i could see layers
of muscle and fat. my neighbor
warns there are foxes here.

i do not tell my neighbor
his cats look wild.   i do not
know my neighbor's name.

iv

there are fears to which
i do not admit.   there are fears
which i refuse to name.   alone

in the dark   i am
afraid of others   but also
of the clean smell

of the refrigerator;
the freshness of chlorine
draws me.   i walk quickly
towards the bedroom.

v

this morning   i cleaned
the yard. i saw a face
from the city   in the trees.

the face was a mask
and i pulled it off
but there was nothing.

vi

patterns in rocks originated from
pressure.   the veins were once separate
stones   pushed together   stamped into
other hard flesh.   they merged
and became ornamental.

                        the colors
blend surprisingly well.   rings
match shapes and textures.   unwilling
inanimate   they played their roles
the iceberg scraping off layers   till
the desired smoothness was achieved.

vii

i do not understand my place
in it.   it seems to have a life
of its own   made by others
simply on loan   for a year

they ask me: how is
your book?   and i give accurate
gas meter readings   wondering
where i will be next year.

the world here is fluid
the beaches undefined.   there are rocks
whose function   i do not know.

edges

1/

the only reason she was not able to make it on her own
though she'd been on her own and alone most of her life
was that she'd never before been forced to distinguish
herself from trees   or sand and sea.   and it became ob-
vious that when it came to rocks   she could never prove
her own distinctness.   the realization   occurring one
very clear   transparent day   when she could see all the
way to the end of the point   frightened her so much   she
ran back to the house and rolled herself up in a blanket.
first   she closed the bedroom door.

2/

the preoccupation with plants   constant watering and hover-
ing over them   checking the buds and fingering the leaves
was another major symptom.   she did not want to admit it
to herself immediately.   she continued watching them some-
times stealthily   hoping she would catch even the minutest
movement.   (she turned the plants away from the sun   and
they turned back.)   it was impossible to catch   to seize
their breath.   she would pretend that when she watered them
the leaves trembled.   but that was fantasy.

3/

though she did not want to mouth it   she knew the words
were missing.   somewhere she'd lost the vocabulary   per-
haps the black night when she pushed herself outside and
down the road   though her hands continued gesticulating
when she ran towards the ocean.   it was a loss she did
not regret   finding it was better to listen   than to manu-
facture.

4/

she could not tell if this was birth or death   moving
out of   or into the grave.   the sand was alternately
hot and dry   and cold and wet   too extreme in either
case   and the ocean took on a different feeling each day
without warning.   in the winter the dune shrubbery seemed
to hold its breath.   she watched it keenly   her eyes
lowered   away from the horizon.

5/

she had kept the seedlings in the bedroom   but that had
become a terrible burden.   she found it impossible to
concentrate and so moved them into the kitchen.   the bed-
room door would remain closed at all times   day or night.
she lived alone   but feared intrusions she could not arti-
culate.   it was not human contact   or human harm.   ra-
ther it was   the kitchen   its smell of food which frightened
her.   it was undefined   and she desperately needed strict
outlines   an unfilled space demarcated.   she chose the bed-
room   keeping the door closed   day and night.

6/

whenever the phone rang she was startled   not because she
didn't expect anyone to call   but because it seemed that here
surrounded by sand   and smell of salt and cooking meat   the
ring was inappropriate.   it was as if some strange creature
had made a demanding noise   insisted on recognition which she
was unwilling to give.   she never knew how to speak   or what
to say.

7/

crushing time between waking and sleeping was a daily con-
cern.   she moved slowly hoping it would move past   post-
poning the waking moment till almost stupor.   it was all
limitless.   seeing the beach fade into the fog   she'd
turn suddenly and discover her footprints had already been
covered by the wind.   no trace at all   as if she'd been
born on that spot in that moment.   she was amazed how
easily markings disappeared and became a part of the shore.
the bluffs stood coldly   eroding.

8/

there had been that moment looking down toward the point
when the horizon had distinctly separated the ocean and sky
and waves came in regular motions   building and collapsing
in unending fury   that she felt herself losing ground   eva-
porating.   she tried to think of the small pale blue flower
which had appeared the day before.   but it was drowned in
the foam which ran towards her toes like soapsuds.   the
water receded   taking the flower with it   and she watched
as she was pushed inland   and the wet sand was pulled away
from her until she felt in one moment it would be too late
and ran back to the house   and rolled herself up in a blank-
et.

9/

the pale blue flower was a surprise.   the plant seemed to
be only leaves.   she had stared at it for a long time try-
ing to remember a word   brack   or bracti   she could not re-
call exactly a lesson she'd once heard.   she was frighten-
ed again.   all this breath   she thought.   she considered
withholding water   that was for a fraction of a second   and
then watered it immediately.   supper had to be cooked.
she checked the bedroom door.

10/

she knew of course that here it would have to be serious
because no one would look in or call   for days   so it was
a serious decision to be weighed carefully   and when fully
sober.   she continued collecting rocks   arranging them on
the deck   planting new seeds   and feeling the scratching
as imperceptible as a forgotten dream   down at the base of
her skull.   she continued cooking   and freezing the food
and answering the phone when it rang   and trying to remember
old words she once knew: viscera   stasis   inchoate.

11/

there was no saving here and no one to advise her and she
really did not want to listen except whether it was acidic
or alkaline   and whether sun was necessary   or humidity   or
if repotting might be helpful for growth   or if fertilizer
had to be used.   she kept taking books out of the library
renewing them   but it was hard to hold it all in.

12/

it culminated in a rage she could not contain.   the door had
not been closed properly   and was pushed open by the draft
from the kitchen   the curtains moved as if breathing in and
out against the screen.   she knew it was too late   and she
could not control it anymore.   she walked to the beach and
scooped up the foam rubbing it against her face.   she squeezed
slimy seaweed   till it squirted strange juices   that trickled
down her legs like green semen.   she walked for a mile collect-
ing all the fish skulls she could find   and arranged them in
concentric circles   placing a rock in the middle.   finally
she carried some large stones to the foot of a bluff   hoping
to prevent erosion.

IV

riverhead: a center*

i

                    it is a training
           center.   children learn
           to sit still   to keep
           fingers out of mouths
           to point to their noses
           socks   to clap hands
      sit still   sit on the toilet
      to bite sandwiches   to keep
      fingers out of mouths   to
      flush the toilet   to drink
from a cup   to point
to hair knees   to sit on command
to sit still
      sit still
         sit still.

              i have come here
         to see myself
         as i glimpsed my image
         one summer   to forget
         your stone eyes
         my inadequacy in them:
         as you turned the page
         and completed the sentence
      so vital   flicking me away.
      these of some other age
      half formed   crepuscular
      creatures   who never recognize
      the sun   touch me deeply
      allow me to return to
myself again.   away from
your marmoreal pose   the spastic
gesture
      springs life.

*In Riverhead, New York, there is a training center for retarded
and disabled children.

it is too much
this pressing against.
              i can't push my words
              into your ears   nor force
              words out of your mouth
nor carve your lifeless
              figure   into an action pose.
              i see you move   from place
              to place: you are at work
now at home   turning
              the page of a book.   all
              patterned   set in a motion
              which defies disturbance.
you guard your mechanism
              carefully: you say   these
              are private things and i won't
              discuss them.   there is
no touching you   though you
              vowed   your eyes big
              moving your head
              back and forth you would
never never   let me go.

              each day is a constant
              repetition of memory and
              gesture: a persistency
                         which appalls   the same
              facial grimaces   twisted postures
              fluttering fingers and high pitched
              ooooooo.   the schedule is pinned
                         to the wall: free play
              bathrooming   attendance   gym
              bathrooming   table work   lunch
              bathrooming   resting   gym
                         and each day   the puzzles
              are distributed   sandwiches broken.
              always the moment of self-
              assertion: refusal to eat   or move
                         followed by a hard slap or disgrace
              behind the door   till tears come
              and the lunch is thrown in the trash.

the same theme   the same applause
                    repeated without boredom
pressed into them so they will not
forget.   and every day they arrive
fresh   unaware of yesterday
its monotony.

iii

          my mother registered
          me in school.   i
cried   holding on to her
leg   screaming i did not want
to go.   already wise
i knew the breach   had been completed
          but it was a scene
          i had to play.

          i rage
          then calmly enunciate
my activities in a tone
revealing: productive.
it is a hollow anger
and you   so impassive
          so arched within
          yourself   are content
to sink into the couch   even deeper
          into the purple velvet
          to cover your eyes and ears
          and mouth   you are content
having speeched prettily of love
of friendship   having fulfilled
the requirements of sound   never
your head moving back and forth
never   to let me go   now focus
          on the vital sentence
          and turn the page.

            one of the boys
            handsome and neat
is a perfect mimic of sounds
and words   but he will never
never talk.   he goes for
religious training
            sometimes he crosses
            himself.

iv

            the supervisor
points to one of the girls
            (she was patterned
for many years   hours and hours
            neighbors arrived
moving her legs and hands according
            to schedule   her brain
never developed   but who knows what
            she would have been
had they let her alone):   if
            we could just
get her to walk with her head
            higher and to stop
drooling   people wouldn't be so
            repelled;   now any
one knows what she is.   the supervisor
            has straight grey
bangs and smiles her easy concern:
            the disgusting habits
must be concentrated on   must be
            eliminated.

                    i have
            never kept the right public
image for you   and privately i've been too demanding
            too volatile   spreading myself
out across your room   insisting intimate knowledge of
            each corner.   but i've seen your face
chalk with sudden fear   your eyes widen with pain.   i've
            seen you lose control
in the gesture of a hand   a turning away to stare
            at a picture on the wall.
we manipulate every moment   refusing to acknowledge
            what we feel.   i am too
crude   and you not crude enough   stubbornly silent
            at critical moments   when one
word would have eased me.   we no longer like
            each other.   we've become
                unsuited.

V

        the place is an armory:
its garage a gymnasium;   off to one side
is a stockroom;   the walls are lined with
        fresh smelling pine clubs
which hang gracefully from clean leather straps;
the metal shelves are filled with blank eyed
        gas masks;   a vault-like closet
contains ammunition.   at the end of the day
the children gather for gym.   some ride tricycles
        some stare blankly at the walls.
any noise from them   is always a relief to hear.
the superintendent of the building   pats them
        on the head as he passes.
occasionally a young soldier stops and says something;
but usually he is embarrassed or visibly repelled
        by their strangeness.

        last night i dreamt
    we met and embraced whispering forgiveness
    for past cruelties.   you held my hand
      i kissed your hair.
    this morning i felt relieved.   i knew it
    was finally completed.   i would stop trying
      to deny the breach.
    we would finish in silence   masked again
    unfamiliar   with our very mouths   hands
      our very veins.

from V

aesthetic distance

only it
can help in the arrangement

: a child   fat
ordinary   except
for its flabbiness
          except
for the bullet hole
through its belly

: a discolored puncture

: a mother (or grandmother
leathered   hard
staring
beyond the bullet hole
beyond the belly

into a dry brown
hard part of this earth

VI

self-dialogues

i.

it seems that you and i
have not talked
now   for a long time
and today   walking by
the gardens   i first noticed
how trees have their own
diseases   cancerous-
like growths that choke
their trunks.

                    once
when i saw a tree cut in half
i said in surprise
it is wet
and you said back:
it is a living thing
and we tend to forget
that like blood
this transparent
dew   leaks life.

i'd forgotten your existence
your heavy boredom in winter
the wetness of life   sitting
here   staring at the incomplete
dry wooden bookshelves   waiting
to be trimmed   sanded
smoothed down from original irregularities
how trees have their own
diseases   that wound
and suffocate with sawdust
their rigid arteries.

ii

today   the day
had no beginning
in the afternoon
i took a walk on the esplanade
and stared at the river.

water is a rare sight
in the city.   you have to search
for it   through secret sidestreets
of elegant neighborhoods
or abandoned factory areas
with punctured windows.   glass
remains a deterrent.

                         but it can
be reached   and from a certain
height   retains a quality
of purity   freshness   though
perhaps it is too tame
too calm today   to reflect its
ocean origins.

iii

it is not a question
of belonging   but rather
of finding a place
and you   are difficult
to place.

the decor of the apartment
has been set   i've worked
hard for the final effect
the position of planters
the colors of the prints
the wall rugs   a feeling
of easy life   with the darker
tones of understanding.

                    frankly
i don't want to disturb
the current scheme   and it is
inconvenient   to say the least
of you to come now   at this time
when i had it all so well arranged
insisting   with your monotony
on the pain.

                  yes yes
pain is a part of life
but i'd prefer
you kept yours
to yourself.

iv

i've recognized you
in the terror-worn
faces of old women
pigeon feeders   who
carry frayed social security
checks   and politely belch
their acid-eaten stomachs
behind their hands.

i've seen you
in the words
of their forced conversations
with young cashier girls
all pink in their
striped uniforms
young girls
who smile   pity
in embarrassment.

i remember how you
used to stand
putting on lipstick.
they also preen
and watch the color run in the cracks
of their skin   and
smear into a wound.
how coquettishly
they prepare
for street society
for passers-by   pulling
down their skirts
over their tired bodies
saying: well someone
will see   and it is always good
to look nice.

i've never liked looking
at them   though i've
stared in pained fascination
thinking of you.

v

i would never have placed
you here   but rather in
some cardboard room   a meager
supply of food in the refrigerator.

and yet i've been lonely
of late   and would not mind
some company   just to fill up
the space.   the livingroom
is lovely this afternoon
light with sun;
some plants are already
beginning to bloom   and
perhaps it might cheer you
to take in the warmth   of the colors
here

i would not mind
such company
that drank in the brightness
and felt my efforts
nourishing.

vi

last night i dreamt i was
a gaunt   and lifeless tree
and you climbed into me to nest.
you were calm   so serious
as you wrapped your legs
around my trunk   and pressed
your body against me.   and
wherever your human skin
touched my rough bark   i
sprouted branches   till
lush with leaves   i grew
all green and silver   frail
like tinsel   holding you
asleep   in my wooden arms.

The Journal of
Rachel Robotnik

THE JOURNAL OF RACHEL ROBOTNIK

> *So all that is in her will not*
> *bloom — but in how many does it?*
> Tillie Olsen, "I Stand Here Ironing"

To the Reader:

Over 10 months ago I received a letter from Ms. Robotnik asking for assistance in editing and finding a suitable place for presenting an excerpt from a journal she had kept while writing her collection of short stories *Kaleidoscope* (Random Books, 1978). She explained that, though pleased with the reception of her work, she had become increasingly uneasy about it. She was "plagued" by the idea that something was missing, and, in hope of pinpointing it, had gone back to her journal from that period. One re-reading made her realize that, though not an integral part of the stories, the journal was a kind of companion piece, almost marginalia, to the fictional work, and she became determined to have it published. She, therefore, asked her editors at Random Books to issue it as a second volume; they refused, as did many other editors over the next year and a half.

Her discomfort over *Kaleidoscope's* acceptance into the literary world, she explained, stemmed from her belief that most reviewers as well as readers could not understand it if they did not understand how it came to be. Hindsight, she wrote me, enabled her to see a sharp difference between the realism of her stories (which had received such praise) and the realism of her journal (which had been rejected) — a difference which she characterized as that between "fairy tales and hard-won vision."

At some point I left one reality for another. It was as if I'd journeyed to another planet. The force of gravity was different. Suddenly I had no grace — was clumsy, awkward, moved with greater difficulty — slow, ever so slow. What amazed me though, was that I never intended to go there, never chose it. Yet there I was and I had no idea how and when I arrived. It was a time without solace, except for those brief moments when I thought about that 'other' place — which gleamed like a dead star whose light I could still see but whose substance, I knew, had long since burned up and vanished.

Anyone familiar with the *Kaleidoscope* stories must agree they are far from fairy tales. Nevertheless, the discrepancy between them and the journal is indeed unsettling. As Ms. Robotnik wrote (and rather bitterly, I think) in another letter:

> Lovers of great art are pure poison. They live for the single moments, for epiphanies, for great revelations. They want to forget what happens in between; they don't want to see the process, the conditions, the dead flies stuck to the half-dry canvas. Yes, they want the journals and the letters — but only after they've been purified of their 'trivia' — only after they are comfortably part of history. Those appreciators of great art — how conscientiously they avoid dealing with the daily grind, how ignorant they are of the real triumph, of the real nature of the tragedy.

From the outset, therefore, we had a tacit understanding that the journal would be edited only for clarity and that no deletions would be made. But remaining completely faithful to the original proved somewhat problematic.

The manuscript covers the period from September 12, 1974 to March 3, 1977, a period during which Ms. Robotnik wrote *Kaleidoscope* and during which she earned her living as a medical transcriber at Memorial Hospital in New York City. It is bound in two black, plastic covers, each containing approximately 175 unnumbered pages. It is typed — extremely unusual for a journal; each entry begins on a new page and is single spaced. Besides the text, it contains numerous *New York Times* articles which are stapled or scotchtaped at the end of entries or on separate pages between entries. Since it was impossible to reprint the articles in their entirety, we decided to provide only the headlines. Underlined passages, however, were reproduced to indicate focus. As will be seen, neither clipping nor labeling (date, page, column) was systematic or consistent.

In addition to the articles, sections from the stories on which Ms. Robotnik was working are occasionally included. These appear three times during the two weeks excerpted here and provide a unique opportunity for comparison with parallel passages in the final version of the title story (pages 7, 4, 19 and 22; hardback Random Books edition).

The text itself contains numerous abbreviations, all of which have been retained. The most frequent are: w/ = with; abt = about; cd, wd, shd = could, would, should; sd = said (used inconsistently); fr = from (used inconsistently); wk = week; $$ = "money," "price," "cost," or "expensive" (used interchangeably); K. = "Kaleidoscope," the story; D = Dia, Ms. Robotnik's lover. Except for "tho" and "thru" I have standardized spelling and corrected obvious slips; words appearing in brackets [ ] are my own, inserted for clarity.

Mary M. Arnold
Chicago
January 9, 1980

Please note: dates in this edition have been altered from the American system to the British system where day precedes month, e.g. 1st June, 1984 : 1/6/'84.

DELAY ASKED IN CURB ON ALIEN PHYSICIANS — New York Hospitals See U.S. Law as Threat to Medical Care — by Ronald Sullivan — A new Federal law that will drastically limit recruiting of graduates from foreign medical schools by hospitals . . .

In New York State, the foreign ratio is much higher, 52 percent, with even higher percentages in municipal hospitals and in those that have no affiliation with a nearby medical school. (5/1; A1)

ECONOMISTS FIND PAUSE ENDING: GROWTH PROJECTIONS FOR '77 RAISED — by Paul Lewis — The recent advance of several important economic indicators has convinced many private American economists that the so-called pause in the nation's economic recovery from the deepest recession since World War II is now ending. . . (6/1; 1)

CALIFORNIA HOMOSEXUALS HELD TO LACK JOB RIGHTS — San Francisco, Jan. 5 (AP) — Homosexuals have no legal protection against job discrimination the California Court of Appeals has ruled. "There is simply no constitutional right [for homosexuals] to work for an unwilling employer . . ." (6/1)

FOR $59, A NEW YORKER WINS A DIVORCE WITHOUT LAWYERS (6/1; 22)

Fri. Jan. 7 '77; 6:30 AM: Windows completely iced over. Feels like I cd freeze to death. Turned on oven. Must call Stan. It's the boiler, *not* the valves. How can anyone so big be so stupid? Einstein was tiny. But then D pointed out Einstein probably cdn't fix the boiler either.

Spoke to Barb last nght. Wants to get together, but too overloaded. [She] Spent fortune on presents. Dead broke. Found it all pointless. So do I. Meeting her nxt Fri at the D[iana].

Claire back yesterday. Combined coffee breaks & lunch & took Roberta to Brew Burger for her 43rd. Outrageous: $52 w/ tip split 4 ways. Limp salads w/ rippled pickles, drinks — & yes, Marcie's $$ diet burger. Long discussion abt *sculptured* nails. Growth & clipping. Gave me the creeps — thought the plastic nails grew. Everyone hysterical. Claire types w/ nails; Marcie w/ fingertips. Both see a manicurist every couple of wks. $15 a visit. Carmen thought it $$. Claire said no — only $1 a day.

BEAME OFFERS PLAN TO CLOSE THE DEFICIT IN 1977-78 BUDGET — Says It Won't 'Sap' Services — 7,500 Job Slots Expected to be Cut — Proposal Needs the Approval of Banks, Unions, State and U.S. (7/1; 1)

PEOPLE'S INAUGURATION TO INCLUDE SOLAR HEATING, BUT NOT FOR MANY (7/1)

Sat. Jan. 8 '77; 6 PM: Dull flat day. Cold. Recyling center. Dragged clothes to laundromat. $$ up again. Shopped. Coffee $$ still impossible. Refused. Tuna on sale (.39). Stocked up. Vowed to make sandwiches for work. Probably won't — too practical. Always forget. D props hers against the door. Vacuumed. Washed kitch flr. Too long.

My turn to call Fla. The same. She's still obsessing he's dirty; he complains she's constantly "rude." Papa's the only person who still uses this word. Both talked abt the strike; disappointed the Steins haven't come down. Leah called last wk & invited them to N.M. [Albuquerque], but Mamma refused. No explanation. More expansive abt kids. Tanya: "remarkable" reading scores. Adam: swimming medal. Best: Alex's article accepted in *CE* [*College English*]. Certain he'll get tenure. So Alex scraped thru. Felt glad for him/them, but found it painful to hear.

Mamma predictably: how are things at the "shorthand pool"? Moved in another direction. She ignored it. I was doing that 15 yrs ago. Isn't there some school I cd be a teacher? Snapped & she w/drew. Know she was hurt — why won't she let it alone? Neither asked abt D. 2 yrs & they still ignore her. What makes it so hard?

D went back early [to her loft] to work on new stretchers. [I] Started organizing for income tx. Hope for $300. Went over mutual expenses for Dec. Our food $$ just flows. Owe D. Didn't get to work till 3 & have to leave in an hr.

Tried working on K. & thinking abt it in some constructive way. Seems unmanageable — no beginning, middle or end — keeps going on & on unfocused. Have no idea what to do w/ all the details. Listed them to see if there's a pattern. A maze. Just don't see the connections.

STRUCK HOTELS BLEAK IN MIAMI DESPITE WINTER SUN — by B. Drummond Ayres, Jr. — . . . The union originally demanded pay increases averaging 10 percent annually plus increased hospitalization insurance and guaranteed tips for some hotel salaries exclusive of tips, run from a low $10 daily for bell-hops to $22 a day for bartenders.
    "I make only $400 a month, half what city lifeguards get," Gilbert Manzano, a Doral Beach lifeguard complained as he walked the picket line in front of the hotel's soaring main building. "I must have dignity."

Sun. Jan. 9 '76 [sic] ; *5 PM:* Ate last night at Sh[ah] B[agh] on E. 6th. Still only place that's kept $$ down. Brought in brandy & got high. Talked abt writing & painting, what it means in terms of "feeling right & complete." & again: how to balance work ($$) & art (work), if it's possible, the general lack of $$ support, grants, etc. D: you can tell how much society values individuality, originality by support it gives artists — just like you can tell how much it values life, human beings by support it gives the poor. I sd it was the same thing. Long discussion. Confessed I've been feeling like a sham lately — unable to complete anything. D asked what schedule I was on. Still *almost* 41 & only 1 collection *almost* completed. Time.

Thought we'd go to the D[iana], but it was after 9 & we didn't want to pay the $3 cover. Felt disappointed. Wanted to dance & see if the Santa & elves mobile was still hanging over dance floor. Walked uptown [to the loft] watching my breath all the way. Empire State [Building] still lit up green & red. Checked for lumber [for stretchers] at M[acy]'s trash bins. Dismantled a display case. Tore my gloves, but got good plywood & 2x4's that wd probably cost $15-20. Extremely exhilarated at getting something for free. Had a sense I cd live just by scavenging. Pictured D & me — old ladies — rushing thru the nght — hugging our loot. Giggled a lot over that. D talked again abt buying a ghost town in Wyoming for $5 & living in the bank.

Back here this a.m. Cdn't concentrate. Kept seeing Quinn in his cubicle peering out at all of us. Then suddenly, my last chart on Fri: the boy w/ sickle cell disease — the neat tables of drugs, dosages, & CBC's — lab tests. The senseless words & statistics: leukocytes, hematocrit, platelets, reticulocytes, lumbar puncture, lymphocytes. Veesey's crisp Indian accent pouring out of the machine: "Bone marrow showed hypo-cellular marrow with many blasts." Thought abt the parents — the long days, the watching for signs.

Don't really understand where all that goes — how I manage to block it out & yet keep it in me, so that if I'm jarred all the pieces fall into place.

Was determined today w/ K. Feel if I don't figure this out, the whole group won't hold & I won't get to anything else. Seems crucial. Must be a form for the lack of focus, the frag-mentation. Retyped list. Not much help. Reconstructed the day I got the toy. Better. Can't articulate the importance, tho I'm moving closer. [I] Remember how Haddley had insist-ed: "Write about what you know!" Seemed obvious at 21. Now the connections, the logic eludes me — a pointless shuf-fling fr place to place, fr house to office, fr task to task. For example: it's hard to absorb at this moment — almost as if it were one of those incomprehensible laws of high-energy physics that I'll actually *live* thru the nxt 5 days, second by second, minute by minute. That I'll be conscious, awake, alive — & yet I know I will.

Each morning I will get up & eat. I will dress. I will talk. I will go to work. I will say hello. I will plug myself into the machine. Time. I will unplug myself from the machine. I will eat. I will talk. I will plug myself into the machine. Time. I will unplug myself from the machine. I will drink coffee. I will plug myself into the machine. Time. I will unplug myself from the machine. I will say good-bye. I will go home. I will be numb. I will be tired. I will be hungry. I will argue. I will make love. I will talk. I will eat. I will watch the news. I will wash my underwear. I will go to bed. I will dream. I will wake up. I will not remember the dream. I will eat. I will go to work. I will plug myself into the machine. And time will pass. And the light will change.

She had never seen anything so wonderful as the patterns in the wooden tube — the endless and effortless regroupings of the colored pieces of glass as they reflected over and over in the angular mirrors. Like the designs formed by the older girls in the maypole dance, she thought after her first glimpse — blue shifting with red and green, then fanning out and allowing the yellow and orange to peek through and then unexpectedly clustering in the center in perfect symmetry.

It had been her mother's gift, presented late one morning when Ania was not quite seven and recovering from her latest bout of a mysterious "lung illness" for which the doctor had no name. Mrs. R. hoped the toy would distract her daughter from the shortness of the visit, and thereby spare her another painful confrontation with the child's loneliness. Rushing into the overheated, shadowy room, the mother was characteristically breathless, appearing unravelled ("not quite put together," her husband had once phrased it), her thick black hair slipping out of its net and her heavy brown woolen coat carelessly misbuttoned.

"I know you thought I wasn't coming, Annushka," she said quickly, upon seeing the gray flecks of anxiety in Ania's eyes. Pointing to the clock on the window sill, she defended herself: "It's only 5 after 11. I'm just a few minutes late. I stopped to get you something." She pulled the kaleidoscope out of the paper bag and immediately saw the child's exhausted fear vanish. This particular toy had once been a favorite of her own and, before handing it to her daughter, the mother stopped for one long extravagant moment to look through it.

"It will remind you of everything beautiful in the world," she murmured almost to herself as she surrendered it to Ania with one hand and placed a thermometer under her tongue with the other. A few moments later, calling from the kitchen where she was preparing Ania's tea and mixing chocolate syrup and milk for Rivka, she added: "You'll never get tired of it. Nothing ever happens twice. As different as snowflakes."

After returning with a tray of two steaming cups of tea and a thick piece of black bread covered with a slice of farmer cheese, she checked Ania's temperature. Relieved it was normal for the ninth day, she began straightening out the tangled quilts and sheets on the makeshift cot, simultaneously instructing Ania to "stay warm and under the covers." Then, in a kind of ritual they had evolved, she proceeded to give the child a bunch of rapid kisses — first one on each eye, then one on each cheek and finally one special one on the tip of her nose — and to press the small face against the rough coat. Quite unexpectedly, as she let her go, the mother added a half-articulate, barely audible excuse: "It's very, very busy today, thank God! Your father needs me." The visit almost over, she now delivered her final orders: "Be sure to nap at one! Drink your tea! Remind Rivka to heat up some soup for you when she gets home! Don't pester her! Wear your slippers when you go to the bathroom! Don't forget to nap!" And she was off — to her husband and the store — more out of breath and less "put together" than when she entered twenty minutes earlier.

It was perhaps the only time during the lonely period of her recuperation that Ania was completely oblivious to her mother's presence, hardly noticing the rapidity with which she executed her duties and disappeared. Extremely susceptible to suggestion, the child allowed the toy to draw her away from the dreariness of her isolation, from the oppressive silence of the bleak apartment, towards everything "pretty" she had ever experienced: the spring maypole festival which she had watched from her friend Alice's room, the sunlight as it leaped at her when she stepped outside, the melody of a song her father sang about the poor shoemaker who worked till midnight and then worked some more. And so forgetting her mother's instructions and her own physical weakness, she sat for hours that day turning the tube till her arms ached and her face was *numb from squinting. She wanted to prove her mother wrong and failed. There was no way to deny the knowledge that none of the patterns would return or "stay put," and with that realization came, for the first time, an acute sense of loss and vulnerability.*

Rivka came home at three. While serving her the bowl of soup, she accidentally bumped Ania's arm so that a particular design she had been trying to balance, suddenly scattered off into the periphery. It did not matter that it was replaced by one equally intricate and fine. Ania was enraged, saying in her most vehement way that she would never, never forgive her. Unaware of her sister's painful discovery, Rivka shrugged her shoulders and told her she had "gone loco." "It would've cracked up anyway," she said calmly drinking her milk. And though Ania knew she was right, knew that her mother was right, she felt defeated for being robbed of a few extra seconds of something so beautiful, so special "that there was only one."

Mon. Jan. 10 '77; 7 PM: Stan just left. Said it was the *thermostat.* Set high enough for the lower floors, not for here. Not allowed to change setting. Was furious. Oven is dangerous. My choice: asphyxiation or freezing to death. He shrugged.

D starts [teaching] new [course] tonight. When I woke up this a.m. she looked calm. Hated to leave the bed, her warmth under the blankets, her skin smooth from sleep. But a wreck all day. Called me 3x fr the center & 2x after she got home. Ostensibly, abt Mr. Antonelli. The same old story: another grossly painted papier-mâché figure of a woman w/her legs spread. Another major speech by Mr. Fernando abt decency in art & the beauty in natural things like birds & trees. Mrs. Stein & Mrs. Sanders indignant, threatening to quit. Robt. promised to speak w/ all of them.

Saw her [D] briefly before she left [for the course]. Don't know why she gets so crazy. Always at the beginning, then the routine sets in — the complaints abt how young they are, how undisciplined. Wonder how it's going. She's probably introducing herself right at this moment.

We tried the new mid-Eastern place last nght. Knew I shdn't, but wanted to get away fr my desk, the sense of failure. Keep saying I'll hold back, then say: what'll I save? $3? $5? What will that get me? So I went. A real rip-off. High $$, small portions. At home, gorged ourselves on Italian pastries.

Feel very close to D right now. There are times when the connection between us is so clear, so obvious, I find it almost painful. When she kissed me last nght, I began to cry. Don't quite know why. Fear? Keep thinking this can't last forever & yet we seem to keep going. Can see her right now — trying to look stern & determined. Never quite pulls it off. Think they realize right away she's a pushover, as soon as she says: "Despite what you've heard to the contrary — art was never meant to be an agony."

AIDES OF CARTER TALK ABOUT JOB FOR MRS. ABZUG — by Frank Lyn — . . . Friends of the former Representative from Manhattan's West Side said that a regulatory agency would be ideal for her since it would give her an independent forum and a minimum of administrative responsibilities. (9/1; 15:1)

NEGOTIATIONS BREAK DOWN IN MIAMI HOTEL STRIKE — Miami, Jan. 8 (AP) — . . . A key union demand is a guaranteed daily tip for maids from each guest staying on pre-paid plans. The union is seeking wage increases of 10 to 13 percent.
Union officials say maids are paid about $16 a day, bellhops $10 a day and food servers about $12.75 a day. All receive tips. (9/1; 26:6)

Tues. Jan. 11 '77; 11 PM: Already overdosed on Quinn & it's only Tues. Seems he'd been to the Coliseum over the wkend for some sort of show & saw 2 midgets there — a couple I presume (why?). Came in this morning, stood in the middle of the room in his shiny blue suit, his hair all puffed up (we heard abt his hair blower last wk) & started describing them: their "wrinkled" faces, the jewelry on their "stubby" fingers. Kept laughing abt how small they were & yet how all their clothes fit perfectly. The woman wore a white fur coat & "cute" leather boots w/ white fur trimming. Everything abt them was "tiny, tiny, tiny." He was impressed by the $$ made-to-order clothes & wondered if they might be circus [people] who earned a lot of $$. Claire sat & tapped her fingers impatiently & Carmen made faces behind his back. Roberta decided she had to go to the bathroom & excused herself rather abruptly when he started describing their skin. But Marcie feigned interest & surprise & kept repeating "You don't say!" Whenever he had his back to her, she'd raise her eyes to the ceiling. Once she gave him the finger.

How was someone like that created? What mother, father, school, neighborhood made him possible? He fills me w/such utter revulsion & hatred. Helpless anger that my life is intertwined w/ his, dependent on him in a bizarre way — all connected w/ the fact that I need to eat. Was left w/ an underlying feeling of nausea — slight imbalance. Took it out on D the second I walked in. The sink was piled w/ dishes & she was pissed because she was ready to go & shop & wanted me to clean up. [I] Just wanted to have a drink & not bother. Suggested we go out. She became furious — on a 23-hour, part-time job & 1 art course she can't afford etc. etc. & neither can I. Knew that, but then she'd been willing to eat out all wkend. Told her I can't keep up w/ what she wants (a lie!).

So we went thru it again. Living in 2 places, neither place ever fully stocked or taken care of. Food spoiling. & *again*: we're not ready to live together, but maybe in the near future, etc. Anyway — *finally* — I did the dishes & she went to 3rd [Ave.]. Made Japanese noodles & fried vegetables. Very good & very cheap. $4 — enough noodles for abt 3 more dinners & some vegetables for one.

Rest of the evening (not much left), she glued paper for drawings & hammered on her stretcher. [I] Worked on K. Thought I got somewhere, tho it still seems very, very lumpy.

Wed. Jan. 12 '76 [sic]; *7 PM:* A scene w/ Quinn & Maurry. Realized that in 2 yrs I've never written abt Maurry. Simultaneously memorable & easy to forget. Probably abt 70, slight limp. Face gaunt, emaciated. Waxy yellowed skin. Sparse hair — stands straight up so even on the calmest day, he looks as if he just came out of a wind-storm. Hard to imagine his evolution — a strange, sweet creature right out of Dickens or Gogol.

His job: to help Terry in the RO [Records Office] across the hall, mainly by running errands, delivering charts, etc. (wd love to see job title & description). Also does odds & ends for Quinn, who's predictably condescending. Calls him "Mr. Maurice," he told Carmen, "to show his respect." Today, for lunch, brought Quinn an $$ hamburger, then went to the RO to eat his own lunch: prefab food consisting of chicken pot pie, chemically compounded pound cake. Suddenly Quinn yelled for him. Came limping in, smacking his lips & twitching crumbs fr his fingertips. Then we heard Quinn quiz him abt the raw onion. There was none & he ordered extra slices & pd for them. So Maurry went out again — in the cold & slush. Didn't seem to mind, tho. Wanted to be obliging. Glad, I think, to be part of a drama (after all, $$ was involved), glad to be of use.

Remember Papa's somber face when he read us "*Bontshe Shvaygt*" [Bontshe Keeps Quiet].* How after a lifetime of being a porter, a non-entity, of being abused, of being hungry, of never complaining — Bontshe finally reaches heaven. Here he can have *anything* he wants. To the angel's horror, he asks only for a warm roll w/ butter. Papa explained: some people have to learn to dream.

> **THE ECONOMICS OF STARVATION II — The Rats Don't Starve — by Emma Rothschild — "We goofed on Bangladesh," one senior official in the Agriculture Department said, "and a lot of people died."**
> **"It was a man-made famine," another United States official said of the Bangladesh famine of 1974. (11/1; 33:2)**

> **NEW HOSPITAL PLAN WOULD CURB LAYOFF — Proposal by Advisory Group Offers an Alternative to the Drastic Cuts Suggested to Ease Deficit — by Ronald Sullivan — A special financial committee that was set up by Mayor Beame has tentatively**

* A Yiddish short story by I.L. Peretz. (M.M.A.)

concluded that the New York City Health and Hospital Corporation can cut its financial deficit without imposing the wholesale job layoffs that were threatened last year. (11/1; 23:3)

DONATIONS ARE URGED BY INAUGURAL PANEL — Plea for $350,000 Is Made to Union Officials and Business Leaders at Fund Raiser in Capital — by David E. Rosenbaum (12/1)

Th. Jan. 13 '77; 10:30 PM: Another bad fight. Had set the alarm early so I cd get up & work. Went off, but I was sleepy & stayed in bed for what seemed only a few minutes. Dozed off. Finally got up & realized it was too late to do anything. So — back to bed. By then D was wide awake, furious. Accused me of *always* setting the alarm & *never* getting up (one of her global statements). Affirmed my right to get up when I felt like it (one of my Bill of Rights statements) whether I actually worked at my desk or not. Pointed out she does a lot of staring at her work & I need time for that too — & I don't get it. Still was defensive. She was tired fr last nght. Had to talk to students & didn't get home till after 11. [I felt] Guilty for waking her & having nothing to show for it. Ended up slamming out of the house. Forgot my lunch.

15 minutes after I got in Quinn told Claire she wasn't typing enough charts. His tallies show she's got the lowest record (big news!) in the pool. In short — told her to shape up. She was in tears — make-up, mascara blotched. Suddenly noticed how rumpled she looked — the knit suit seemed worn & ragged — not her usual clean & prim image. Worn-out. Older. & of course she *is* older, at least 15 yrs older [than Q]. Took some bus[iness] c[ourses] in man[agement] or something as an under[graduate] & now he's a damn super[visor] over a woman who cd be his mother.

Claire's sure he'll fire her. But Carmen sd he's never fired anyone in the last 4 yrs — & quite a few weird ones had passed thru — too chicken — a real old fashioned bully, i.e. coward. Claire pretty shaken tho. Cindy sick last wk — lost 2 days — no $$. & she's worried Bert will cut off support. Been complaining the payments are too much, asking what she does w/ the $$ & how come Cindy's not dressed "more pretty." She's not sure if he's just hassling for kicks, or if he really intends to cut down/stop the $$. Have no idea how much is involved. Can't be much, tho — he's working in a gas station. Still any $$ makes a difference.

We were all upset & had lunch together. Claire, nervous & defensive: she's been typing a lot of foreigners & it slows her down (added she's not sure she types more than any of us). Roberta: we shd keep our own records & hand in the same # of charts, at least the same # of pp. Carmen: still not fair since the A[mericans] go faster than the others. Frustrating & tense. Marcie conspicuously silent — picking at her jello & cottage cheese. Sd a couple of wks ago she wants to push so she cd ask for more $$. [I] Wanted to ask how she felt abt equalizing, but somehow cdn't. & it's true. Claire *is* the slowest one, which clearly means she shd be stood against the wall & shot.

The whole thing felt very delicate & nothing was resolved. It wd help if the drs. bothered to enunciate, but they barely go thru the motions & the A[mericans] are often as hard as the others. Just mumble, suck candy & eat snacks. Assume we'll get what we need in the charts. Time.

When I got home D sd she'd been evaluated at the center. Her *1st* time, so she was completely unprepared. Robt. gave her grades! She's 45 yrs old & she got grades! All A's & B's — rapport w/ workshop members: A-. We cracked up over Mr. Antonelli. Got 1 C: efficiency in filling out forms. Cdn't believe it! We were both in stitches.

Made no reference to this a.m. Won't set the alarm for tomorrow tho tempted. Don't want a repeat performance & I'm exhausted. Enough issues for one day. Am I intimidated?

After supper made lunch. Worked well for a couple of hrs. K. still in sections — unresolved, but some progress.

HENRY FORD 2nd QUITS FOUNDATION, URGES APPRECIATION FOR CAPITALISM — by Maurice Carroll (12/1; A4)

FROM GROWER TO TABLE, COFFEE WILL COST MORE — by Rona Cherry — Despite the growing boycott of coffee in the United States, some industry analysts expect prices to rise steadily at least until early 1978, perhaps reaching $4 a pound in stores. (12/1)

UNEMPLOYMENT DROPS AND JOB TOTAL RISES: WHOLESALE PRICES UP — December Rise 0.9% — Volatile Farm Sector Jumps, but Industrial Goods Climb the Least in 7 Months — by Edwin L. Dale Jr. — Jobless Rate at 7.9% — 3 Million More at Work by End of Year after a Spurt of 222,000 in December — by Edward Cowan (13/1; 1)

ETHNIC GROUPS ANGERED BY PLANS FOR CARTER'S 'PEOPLE'S' INAUGURATION, FEELING LEFT OUT — by Bernard Weinraub (13/1)

Fri. Jan. 14 '77; Midnight: Mamma called. [I] Became very frightened. Late — 11:30. But everything's all right. Just keeps ranting — he's dirty — a filthy man! Asked what was dirty abt him. Everything — stains his shirts & leaves spots & hair in the bathtub. Got nowhere. Is she having a breakdown?

Can't understand it. All those yrs of talk abt retirement — their only dream. Wd never look at cheese again, hated the store — the dampness & cold — cdn't wait to get rid of it. At least that's what *she* said. Wanted warmth, sun, late morning hrs. & tonight: "You don't know how he is, how he *really* is. Dirty. Dirty on purpose." Told her to try & relax, pointed out she never thought that before. Classic reply: she'd been too busy to notice — was seeing him "properly right" for the 1*st* time. Then she cried how she tries to keep the apt. clean & how he messes things up & she *must* have order. Just don't understand her. Didn't know how to respond. Think it's strange she called me & not Leah. Apparently been trying to reach me all evening. [Phone] Ringing when I walked in.

Dinner w/ Barb — good! Met for a drink at the D[iana]. Holiday decor dismantled. Reminisced abt the 1*st* time she brought me there. My confusion because I didn't know (a) if we were on a date; & (b) if everyone in the place was a dyke. Was dumbfounded that so many women looked "perfectly straight." Expected to see a bar full of bull dykes in leather & chains. It was crowded tonight, women coming directly fr work, wearing their working clothes. Increasingly aware of how young they seem. It's unusual to see anyone over 40, almost never over 50.

Barb's doing ok — tho very lonely. [She] Concedes it's a relief to come home & not face one of Annie's numbers. Difficult Xmas — Annie conspicuously absent fr the family dinner. No one asking any questions. An eerie family silence around the break-up.

The usual talk abt work & $$ & the lack of it. But big news: Barb came out at school. Sd she's been nervous & edgy, kids really getting to her. Wanted someone to know what was going on. Thought of course everyone knew by now. Told Anita, who was completely stunned. Funny — Barb's been thru the whole trip — someone I know, a friend of mine, this woman I know, my roommate, the woman I live w/. Still total shock when they finally hear: *lover, lesbian*. Felt envious. Wish I cd bring myself to do it — at least w/ Carmen (does she know, *really* know?). Maybe Roberta wd cut the jokes abt Quinn. Why can't I do it? What stops me? Barb sd I'll do it when I'm ready. When?

Feel anxious. Wish D were home. Don't like her seeing Lisa. Hate straight snobs. Always a toss up abt why they're looking down at you at any specific moment.

Weekend: Taxes. K. Movie w/ Barb tomorrow nght.

Sat. Jan. 15 '77; 10 PM: Mamma called this a.m. Told Papa to move out & he went to a hotel a few blocks away. Perfect timing. Strike's over. "He's wasting all our $$," she told me. Asked her how she expected him to live in a hotel & not spend extra $$. Ignored me & complained I always side w/ him (that's probably true — why?). The crisis: he spilled something (tea?) on the new tablecloth w/ lace trimming. Adamant he'd done it on purpose. "These things are not accidents." So she told him to get out. [I]

Was tongue-tied — asked her if she felt ok abt spending the nght alone (don't think she's ever done it before). Sd she's "an adult woman" & "it's abt time I shd be on my own." Will call tomorrow. Called the hotel. He sounded extremely tired but ok. Just wants some peace & quiet to read his paper. Sd the bed seemed comfortable, that it was "puffed up looking."

Felt frustrated. Want to side w/ her, or at least feel her side (see it very clearly), but something always stops me. Know she's given up so much for him. But she's so impossible — a broken record, a memorized chant. Can't get past the formula, can't reach the pain. Her rage — why does it put me off so? He's of course, stoic & silent. & there I am: stone.

Started crying the second I put the phone down — like a kid whose parents are abt to divorce & has to choose. Remember how D felt when her parents died — an orphan at 42.

D thought we shd stay home in case one of them called — cancelled w/ Barb. Invited her for dinner, but she wanted to try the D[iana] alone. Sounded disappointed. D wcnt down & bought brie & brandy & food for dinner. Turned the kitchen upside down, used all the dishes. Created an elaborate 10-step chicken curry casserole. Sat around & drank while it was in the oven.

Swapped stories abt our parents, what kept them together. Am constantly amazed how outside our parents we are — outside the bond, the intimacy — in a way we're not w/ friends or even other relatives. How strange to live in a home w/ a secret that will never be revealed. My parents were together for 44 yrs & at this moment he's in a hotel & she's in an apt alone — & except for the obvious I don't have a clue. Maybe there's nothing more than the obvious.

Feel tired & drunk. Started out as the usual Sat: recycling center, etc. Then Mamma's call. Didn't get a chance to do laundry. Now I'll never catch up on the wk. D stayed all day. [I] Was glad, but also guilty — neither of us did any real work. There's no time to be human.

It came after a long, undefined illness when she was seven years old — something to do with a lung "weakness" inherited from a Russian grandmother who had died of tuberculosis. Mrs. R., who still retained vivid memories of her mother's deathbed, now agonized over having passed on the genetic defect. Each day she watched in terror as the doctor came and felt the hot forehead, listened to the rumbling in the fragile lungs, and puzzled over the fever which refused to be exorcised by penicillin.

When she saw she was ill, Mrs R. immediately removed Ania from the bed she shared with her older sister and placed her on a makeshift cot created by two overstuffed armchairs facing each other. These she moved near the living room window, close to the steaming, clanging radiator and within arm's reach of the couch where she and her husband slept. For three weeks she sat and watched as the child, lost in a maze of feverish dreams and oblivious to her own danger, diminished visibly in size and sank deeper and deeper into the thick quilts and puffy pillows. It seemed an illness without an end — a futile struggle to force some food into the frail body that consistently refused sustenance.

In addition, there was another worry. Rivka was losing weight and beginning to cough. Her skin looked faded, sallow. The anxious mother consulted the doctor who found nothing wrong. Rivka had managed to contract the symptoms but not the disease. Mrs. R. diagnosed the problem herself one afternoon when she saw her older daughter's face a moment after she had been told to stay out of the living room. It was simple and there was nothing to do about it. She had to nurse the sick one. He had to be in the store. Rivka would have to make do.

*****

But as soon as Mrs. R. became convinced the fever was banished permanently from her daughter's body, she was once again immersed in the details of the store and in the seemingly hopeless battle to pay off the debts incurred during Ania's illness. Initially, Rivka was kept home from school to watch over her "baby" sister. Though only a year older, she was an adept nurse, reheating soup, making fresh tea and concocting a special "goggel-moggel" — milk heavy with honey and melted butter. In addition, she was good at telling endless stories about Smelly Fanny, Ania's second grade teacher, and her inept solos at Wednesday assembly. But after a week, when Ania's recovery seemed to have "taken hold," Rivka was ordered back to school and Ania was left alone, staring silently at the clock.

If the illness did not change her, the recovery did — a painful period of confinement and isolation which allowed her to focus on her surroundings for the first time. She quickly developed a kind of aversion to her own home, an unspoken anger at her parents. She did not, of course, articulate it that way. What she expressed was more of a feeling, an uneasiness, which had suddenly made her wary. She complained to her mother that she felt dizzy, that she thought she might fall over, that the sidewalk was unsteady, and repeatedly asked if there were a "safe place" to go to. Mrs. R. now began to worry whether the extended fever had not left a serious mark on the child who, though the doctor said had reached perfect health, insisted "the world is crooked and makes me sick." Things were "tipped," she said angrily, tipped so she might slide right off. She thought about Columbus, how he went on his voyage unafraid he might "hit the edge and fall off." Maybe — Ania argued with her father — just maybe, Columbus never reached the horizon. How could anyone be sure? Maybe it was still there — waiting.

Sun. Jan. 16 '77; Noon: 1st thing, called Mamma. Very distant. Doesn't like how I talk to her. Thought I'd understand because of my "women's ideas." Asked if all that applied to everyone else. Told her [that] wasn't the point. Almost hung up — sd she needed to vacuum the apt. Coaxed her: talked abt the cold wave, the wind-up of the strike, plants, Mrs. Kravitz's singing. [She] Said it's been quieter lately.

Then Papa: very depressed, somewhat disoriented — doesn't have his things around him. "Do you think she's gone crazy?" he asked. Said I didn't know, but thought perhaps she was very tired & just didn't want to wash another tablecloth.

Finally braced myself & called Leah. Instant hysteria. Kept saying: "I just can't believe it! I just can't believe it!" Promised to call them tonight & me tomorrow. Felt sorry for her — how they neglected her, for work, for $$ — made her into the little automaton mamma she is today — & now they can't stand to be in the same room. Keep seeing Mamma at the sink, her red hands wringing out the damn table cloth, the tight gray bun, the tight lips — no loose ends, no strands. When did she pull herself in like that?

Totally drained by the calls. Bitched to D the whole wkend was shot, K.'ll never get finished. She casually suggested I quit. Go on unemployment or get a loan (where?) & focus on my writ[ing]. Haven't done that since I got this job. 2 yrs of my life. Seems longer. D thought the business w/ Claire was a set-up. It's possible Quinn's budget's been cut & he's being pressured to fire someone. Hadn't occurred to me, but if it's true, then maybe he'd be content to get rid of me.

Was excited for abt 30 sec — then filled w/ complete, utter panic. To go on unemployment w/ no savings of any sort. I've been thru that — the constant hustling — on the books, off the books. Always trying to be 1 step ahead, at least 1 month's rent ahead. Constantly at the mercy of the phone, unable to turn down any shit job that comes along because there's never any guarantee there'll be another one later. So ultimately the writing came last anyway. I hated, *hated* living like that — never sure where I'd be nxt — no schedule, no order, no routine — working 1 month in the evening, the nxt in the morning. That's why I'd gotten this job. It's steady. It's predictable. It's secure.

But D insists my priorities are all wrong. My writing shd come *1st* — & if I can grab 9 mos. of even marginal existence, I shd. Sounds very reasonable, perfectly sensible. But then overwhelming breathless fear — like running on a floating piece of ice — & suddenly reaching the edge.

Had hoped, wanted desperately to escape this. Can still see Mamma & Papa going [over] accounts & monthly $$, the rent *almost*, but not quite pd. Mamma begging, then insisting Papa [call] Uncle Joe & [borrow] $$. He refusing because Joe was younger & his pride wdn't let him. Then he'd leave the table, his food only half eaten, his face set hard, spitting out the words: "I deserve to eat in peace!" & Leah — ashen — [her] fingers clutch[ing] at [her] skirt, pleading w/him to come back. Always during dinner — till my stomach was a knot fr anxiety abt the numbers coming [out] right, balanc[ing]. The same knot tonight at the prospect of not [being] able to get thru the month, feeling I'm in a race w/ my checkbook. & the less I have, the more frantic, reck[less] I get. Like Mamma before the maypole dance. How strange she seemed — her voice from somewhere deep inside her: "The few dollars, Jake, what's the difference? For God's sake! Let them have the dresses!"

BEAME CUTS CITY COFFEE BUYING BY A 3rd — by Edward Ranzal — The soaring price of coffee has added to the city's fiscal headache. Mayor Beame yesterday ordered a one-third cut in the purchase of coffee ordered by the city for its hospitals, prisons and other institutions. (14/1; B3)

20-DAY MIAMI HOTEL STRIKE SETTLED — . . . Last week the union was said to have dropped the pre-paid tip demand, but the issue of rehiring the striking workers had not been settled until today.

Union members, most of whom are Cubans, are expected to approve the agreement, as recommended by the union leadership. (15/1)

NEW ECONOMIC SLUMP FOR INDUSTRIAL NATIONS IS FEARED — by Clyde Farnsworth. (15/1)

Mon. Jan. 17 '77; 7:30 PM: Barb called last night to ask abt my parents. Brought her up to to date. Told her D's idea abt unemployment (wonder if D's right abt Quinn). Supportive. Asked what I was saving for. Sd I wasn't saving at all. B: "What's the point? You can always get a job like that." Can I? Took me 3 mos. last time. Thought she was glib.

[She] Lasted exactly ¼ hr at the D[iana].Sd the average age was abt 25 & the whole scene made her feel old, worn out, lonely. Thought the younger women just turned off when they looked at her. Told her she's paranoid, but secretly empathized.

It wd scare me to be alone again. When did we become "older dykes"?

David called at the office & sd he'd stop by to have lunch nxt wk. Genuinely shocked abt my parents. Sd he always loved the store & that Papa used to give him extra chunks for treats. Still remembers the crumbs of farmer cheese sticking to his fingers. But he saw it fr the outside. I remember Mamma's rage. "You feed other people's children better than your own," she once said. Have no business giving away food — like giving away $$. "How come," she once taunted, "you're suddenly so big-hearted?" Was she right? Can't find the center.

Bumped into Annie on the way home fr the subway — 1st time in months. Felt guilty for never calling her. Unemployment up in 3 wks (I clutched). [She] Asked if I knew of any work. Told her I'd think abt it — gave her Sally & Ruth's number. [She] Sd the 9 months had been productive, but rough. Took a lot of pictures. Asked if D & I are planning to live together. Said *no* — there are different ways of being together. Felt defensive. Also somewhat awkward. Know there's always 2 sides, but do think she was unnecessarily cruel to Barb. Never really understood it, because I'd never perceived her that way before they started having problems. But as soon as that began, she seemed to become someone else. Yet today, on the street, she seemed the old Annie.

Tues. Jan. 18 '77; 10 PM: Ironic? Bad fight w/ Quinn. Maybe I *can* get him to lay me off. Came in this a.m. & asked to see me. Checked what I'd done yesterday & told me to change my typewriter ribbon. [I] pointed out he saw only the carbons. He nodded. So I sd: "You mean to tell me you can look at carbons & know my original is too light?" He became enraged, started pounding the desk — reminded me he was running things. Became frightened, thought he might try to hit me. Left feeling very shaky.

Called D later in the afternoon. Told me to ignore him — just do what I have to & think abt leaving — either getting unemployment or another job — it's not the only hospital that needs transcribers. She sounded irritated, had just gotten home fr the center — only a couple of hrs. left of daylight.

Seemed depressed & distant when I got home. Sd she feels I'm never satisfied, that she doesn't provide me w/ anything. Felt caught off guard. Told her she was absolutely wrong, that our relationship is extremely important. At the same time, thought that *the relationship is not everything*. It doesn't, can't help me w/ certain things, can't ease my frustration that I'm not doing what I want. Sometimes — today — when I'm so stuffed w/ that idiot at the office, so empty of my own self, I wonder who it is she cares for so much. Is it really me?

Feel stymied abt how to save myself, how to hold on to myself. Am afraid I might drive D away. Am so eaten up w/ anger & bitterness that sometimes I don't recognize who I am. *Know* that I must come to terms w/ **$$** & my work. *Know* also that maybe there's really no solution, that this is the way it's going to be, no matter how much I rage. Feel as if I've been pounding my head against a brick wall & finally am beginning to *know* for the first time, that there is no way out — there are no real choices, that the opportunities are narrow, limited. *Know* for the first time that all those dreams, those fantasies, abt who I'll be, what I'll be, will simply not come true. Keep seeing the broken toy — the translucent pieces of colored glass all at the bottom of the tube, lumped together in a dark, opaque heap. The mirrors cracked — no pattern, no design.

Apologized repeatedly to D. Made her dinner. We talked a lot abt our expectations, how to make them realistic. It was good. D grounds me.

ANAIS NIN, AUTHOR WHOSE DIARIES DE-PICTED INTELLECTUAL LIFE, DEAD — by C. Gerald Fraser — . . . In addition to the diaries' pictures of the Bohemian and intellectual life of Paris in the 1930's and of New York during and after World War II, her journals became widely known for their view of the perspective of a Western woman and artist struggling to fulfill herself.
 . . . . Her life, she said, "covers all the obscure routes of the soul and body, seeking truth, seeking the anti-

serum against hate and war, never receiving medals for its courage. It is my thousand years of woman-hood I am recording, a thousand women. It would be simpler, shorter, swifter not to seek this deepening perspective to my life and lose myself in the simple world of war, hunger, death." (16/1)

FIVE-DAY 'PEOPLE'S' INAUGURATION BEGINS IN CAPITAL TUESDAY — by Bernard Weinraub — . . . the inauguration planners are emphasizing the 'simplicity' of the day.

For example, the President-elect will wear a business suit rather than the morning coat and top hat traditional for the event. For lunch on Inauguration Day, the families of Mr. Carter and Vice-President Mondale will eat sandwiches, buttermilk, and fruit . . .

Inauguration Day starts at the Lincoln Memorial at 8 AM Thursday with an interfaith prayer service . . . (16/1)

Wed. Jan. 19 '77; 12:30 PM MH [Memorial Hospital]: No word fr Leah. Suppose it's terrible, but I didn't call her. Spoke to Fla before going to bed. Both the same. They'd talked w/ Leah Sun nght.

Went w/ the others to the cafeteria. Food looked so disgusting (called "chicken chow mein") — goppy, gooey stuff — abt 3 shreds of chicken — took one look & my stomach flipped. How can hospital food be so awful & so unnutritious? It's all corn starch & chemicals. So bought an apple & coffee & came back. Didn't want to spend the $$ anyway. Have started a writing fund — i.e. will try to save some $$. Tx refund shd help. Too wiped out yesterday & this a.m. to make lunch. *Must* get myself to do that. End up spending abt $15/week in the lousy cafeteria — almost $60/month. Cd use some of it for vacation & some of it for my writing fund — don't have to give it to that place. Why are all the daily mechanics, the little details so draining, so costly? Why am I not more disciplined? Why am I always forced to choose between time & $$, when time is $$, so I'm always losing?

Quinn tried to be friendly this a.m. Nodded but didn't stop typing. Later asked him abt W-2 forms. Polite, sd he'd ask. He's trying to improve relations. Carmen talked to him abt a point system, so we cd get credit for the more difficult drs. Claire's pushing. Sometimes I can't bear to look at her, the concentration, the anxiety on her face. Can always tell when she's stuck, hearing the tape click again & again as she goes over the same words. & Marcie's just as determined to get her extra $$. Know she's got a right, but sometimes I'm so angry w/ her. Makes no sense. Am angry w/ the wrong one.

It was as if she realized for the first time that the life she was born into was not universal. There were people who did not live in dingy basement apartments, so that all they saw was the strewn garbage on the street. A home was not always three damp, dark rooms. The couch in the living room was not destined to open every night for parents to sleep in, while the two daughters crowded in a narrow bed in the room facing the alley. Not all daughters were exchanged for necessity. All these things, she was beginning to understand, did not have to be.

Yet why, how had this particular life come to her? Was it a legacy like the weakness in her body? Was it an accident? Had it all simply fallen into place randomly? Could it be swapped? Altered? Could the world be jostled so that it formed a different pattern for her? Was it possible, perhaps, to wake up in her friend Alice's sunlit room high on the eighth floor overlooking the park and peer down to where the girls danced around the maypole, weaving their long, brilliant ribbons and forming patterns she could never have discerned from the ground? In short, was there a way to open her eyes one morning and find herself inside another life?

The question was both dream and nightmare.

Thurs. Jan. 20 '77; 6:00 AM: Leah finally called last night. Total panic. Kept saying: "What's going to happen? They can't do this! They just can't do it!" Tried to calm her, told her it might be better if they separated for a while. Mamma hasn't had a chance to realize the consequences. Tried to comfort her, but am very anxious. Don't like to think of them isolated, envision something happening, something physical. Tripping & falling — unable to reach a phone. Am scaring myself, but have always assumed they'd be there for each other (for me?). Leah sd Mamma's still talking abt $$ he's spending. Papa's resigned — eating in the hotel dining room & taking walks. Uncle Joe saw him yesterday. Leah sd Papa was crying. Hard to imagine.

We discussed the possibility of one of us flying down there. Leah implied it shd be me since I have "fewer responsibilities." Meaning: no husband or children — you're obviously free. Growled silently. Wanted to say: I also don't get paid if I don't show up for work! Felt the old rage: a job, a lover, my writing, *my life*! None of that counts. I'm the unmarried daughter — always available, always on call.

D sd Leah's very threatened by it all: "After all, we're the ones who're supposed to have the unstable lifestyle." Probably true. Thought I shd refuse to go, that I just cdn't afford it. I snapped that was easy when it was theoretical. Regretted it the second it was out of my mouth. Knew it wasn't true. Apologized. Feel this is a maze w/ no exit. We finally went to bed. Held on as if I were drowning.

Bad, bad insomnia. Kept thinking abt Leah & Mamma & Papa & the store & what we all looked like 30 yrs ago — the old faded photographs. Who wd have predicted it, any of it? & then kept dozing off & dreaming vaguely abt Quinn — not really able to remember it. & I'd wake up & think abt leaving & writing & the $$. & shd I do it? & cd I do it?

This a.m. got up w/out the alarm at ¼ to 6. Freezing. Exhausted. Decided I might as well get up & write. It's as good a time as any.

COLDWAVE CONTINUES TO GRIP EASTERN U.S. — Two Elderly Men Die of Exposure in Hotel on Amsterdam Avenue — by Peter Khiss — Two men in their 60's were reported by the police in the West 151st Street station to have died during the day at the Hudson Residence Hotel, 1649 Amsterdam

Avenue, at 141st Street, because of exposure to the cold. The Police had been told that heat had been only sporadic in the building for several days. (19/1; 1:4)

Keeper of Accounts

For Judy Waterman

Acknowledgements

I am very grateful to my mother Rose Perczykow Klepfisz for volunteering financial support that enabled me for a period of time to focus entirely on my writing. In addition, I am indebted to Frances Hanckel, executor of Claudia Scott's estate, for other financial assistance made available through a provision of Claudia's will. As a result of their generosity, I was able to extend a planned writing period of three months into eight.

The eight months, when I was completely free from income-producing work, proved to be very productive. At the beginning of the summer of 1981, only the two "Monkey House" monologues (1976-77) and "Contexts" (1979) existed in completed form. The "Work Sonnets" were in rough draft (without the Notes or the Monologue) and the series "Urban Flowers" was only partially finished. Started well over a year and a half earlier, both were completed during this time. In addition, I began and finished "Glimpses of the Outside," *Bashert*," and "A Poem for Judy/beginning a new job." Towards the end of this period, I began to think about another poem that ultimately emerged as "Solitary Acts"; but this took almost five months to complete because I had already returned to full-time work.

I feel it important to give this history of how *Keeper of Accounts* came to be written not only because I am grateful to my mother and Frances for making it possible, but also because I want to remind myself and others of the circumstances that are most conducive to creative work. A block of uninterrupted time—unencumbered by a job or financial anxiety—is critical to every form of creativity and rarely available to most of us, especially to those of us who are out of the mainstream. I feel particularly fortunate to have received it in these times of economic depression and do not want it to be taken for granted.

Irena Klepfisz
October, 1982

I. From the Monkey House and Other Cages

From the Monkey House and Other Cages

The voices are those of female monkeys born and raised in a zoo.

Monkey I

/1/

from the beginning
she was always dry   though
she'd press me close
prying open my lips:

the water warm
the fruit   sour   brown
apples bruised and soft.

hungry for dark   i'd sit
and wait   devour dreams
of plain sun and sky
large leaves   trunks   dark
and wet with sweet thick sap.

                but morning
brought back the space
and cement   her weakened
body   my head against her
breast: my mouth empty.

yet she was   all
my comfort: her sharp
ribs against my cheek
her bony fingers   rough
in fluffing me dry.

she showed me   all
the space   the changing
colors outside   then

pulled me back   forced
me to sit with her
in a shadowy corner.

on certain clear days
she'd shrug   hold me in the sun:
her fur lacked smoothness
her body warmth.

/3/

in the midst of heat
they took me   with smooth
round strokes   and hushing
sounds.
          she sat silent
at first   sniffing their sweat
their stale breath   then leaped on one
her eyes wide   her claws poised and sharp.
          he grunted   deep
from within   an empty cavern
echoing the storm outside
flicked her off   and dragged me out.

i could hear her sound
as if a sea lion roared
then becoming tired
                    drowned.

/4/

their space was smaller
cramped and low   the air
foul   with their sweat
their salt.
            and their motions
were sharp   as they spread me out
clamped me down
for the opening probe.

                  i did not move
just sucked my breath
with each new venture   into my deepest parts
and then   with time
i became   a dark dull color
a gray rain   blending
with the liquid   of her eyes.

/5/

when they returned me
the air was ice:
bare branches   meshed
against a hard   dark sky.

i sat alone.   we were
separate now   though
she was still there
in the cage   next to mine.
her fur was stiff   her nostrils spread
she eyed me   circled
her back arched   ready for attack.

later   as the food was dropped
she leaped forward
hissed   snatched bits of fruit
from my side   of the bars.

a day   and a day
the pools   dead and dry
i'd sit and stare
into the cold   into the empty trees.

but she seemed   at rest
pressing against the bars
eyes closed   alone   on the other side.
only when i ate   she'd look sharp at me
her mouth moving
as i swallowed   each bite

and as night blackened us
she'd gather her scraps
enclose herself   in her arms.

/7/

the male   sleek-furred
was young   and active
when they forced him through to me.

i stayed in place   all
eyes and ready   while she leaped
in frenzy   retreated to the furthest wall.
he kept his distance
ignoring her   ignoring me
ate small morsels   tumbled
stared outside.

the ice was thawing
the pools filled and quiet.
i listened   as the soil
sopped   became mud
deep   and brown.

soon the trees budded   and i
pinked   softened   and presented.
he penetrated   withdrew
penetrated   withdrew
over   and over
till i was dry
and hard.
       she sat
relaxed and quiet
began to chew apples
slowly picking out
each black seed.

                    later
i cramped   shrivelled
then opened   wide   wide
my flesh thin and stretched
till: it burst forth
a thing   so strange
so pale   and hairless
a mass of flesh   separate from mine.

and through the heat
and heavy trees   the sound of water
the light of the moving sun:
the male ate regularly
the small one sucked
i mashed the sour fruit
between my lips.

she watched us all
as we would swallow
hoard   any piece of rind
or seed   that she could find.

the male was taken:
i turned my back.
the small one was taken:
i was held to one side.

and again   and again
the trees emptied again
the soil became hard
then became soft again.

and the cage is   all
mine   and i have myself:
touching my fur
pulling my face

while she moves so slowly
without any sound
eating   pacing
twisting her arms   around the hard bars.

sometimes at night   i watch
her asleep: the rigid bones
the thinned out fur

and i can see clearly
the sky   the bars
as we sat together
in a spot of sun
and she   eyes closed
moved me
moved me
to the sound of the waters
lapping
in the small   stone pools
outside.

Monkey II

/1/

to state each horror
would be redundant.   the objects
themselves suffice: a broken comb
an umbrella handle   a piece of blue
plastic   chipped pocket mirror.

the face is unfriendly.
i try to outstare it   but
it persists   moving

spastically   the eyes
twitching   open   shut
nose quivering   wrinkled fingers
picking at the ears.   i do not know

this stranger.

/2/

i have heard of tortures
yet remain
strangely safe.

        but at night
i am torn by my own
dreams   see myself live
the grossest indignities   probes

and unable to rip myself from my flesh
i remain silent   not
uttering sound   nor moan   not
bothering to feel pain.

waking   in early light
alone   untouched
i cry over my safety.

/3/

when they first come
they screech with wildness
flinging themselves against the wall
and then against the bars.

some sit and cry for days
some   never recover and
die.
        they are familiar
yet crap uncontrollably   plead
shiver and rock.   i refuse

to have anything to do with them
till they learn to behave.

/4/

at her arrival   she was
stunned and bruised.   she
folded up   refusing to eat

her mouth grim.   i staked
out my territory   recognizing
her fierceness   her strength.

but she weakened   grew sick
was removed without resistance
returned three days later
shaved patches on her arms.

later she told me: we create
the responses around us.

i remember the grasp of her claws
the vicious bite   the scar
still on my leg.   she was crazed

jabbering   then attacking
again.   and the sun seemed to fall away
into coldness   as i pressed myself
against the corner   the hardened sand
under my nails.   i began to gnaw
through concrete   my face raw.

they took her away
and when she came back
she did not look at me.

/6/

scatter yourself
i told her   moving
myself into the left
corner   where i sat
observing the movement
of her head.

                she nodded
seemed to sleep
then stood up   pointing
outside.   the leaves were
red.   it was a falling time
noisy   dry twigs cracking
off nearby trees.   i felt

content   watching myself
while she pointed   the leaves
red.

          and finally
she said   this is enough
and began to bang her head
against the wall   one thud

after another thud   she batted
herself beginning to bleed
throwing herself and falling.

they came   and tried to seize
her   while the sun vanished
and the trees   moved slowly

and everyone   so still
afraid to breathe: the moon
all fresh   and the birds
small balls of feathers.

i puked as they dragged her out:
tufts of fur on the stone floor.

/8/

when she died   i mourned
a silent mourning.
                              and
the others asked
asked   asked
and poked at me.

there had been much between us
in gesture.   mostly i remember
her yellowed teeth   her attempt
at tameness.

there had been no sound:
just the motion of   our hands
our lips sucked in
toes pointed   outward.
it had been enough.

                    dizzy
with messages   i would lie
down   dream of different
enclosures.

II. Different Enclosures

Contexts

for Tillie Olsen

> "Dollars damn me."
> —Herman Melville, as cited in *Silences*

> "I have no patience with this dreadful idea that whatever you have in you has to come out, that you can't suppress true talent. People can be destroyed; they can be bent, distorted, and completely crippled."
> —Katherine Anne Porter, *ibid.*

I.

I am helping proofread the history
of a dead language. I read out loud
to an old man whose eyes have failed
him. He no longer sees the difference
between a period or a comma, a dash
or a hyphen, and needs me for I under-
stand how important these distinctions are.

The room is crammed with books, books
he had systematically tagged for future
projects—now lost. Sounds pour out
of me. I try to inject some feeling
and focus, concentrate on the meaning
of each linguistic phrase. On the edge
of my vision, he huddles over a blurred
page, moves his magnifying glass from line
to line, and we progress. Time passes.
My voice is a stranger's, sensible and
calm, and I, the cornered, attentive hostess,
listen in silence as it conjectures the his-
tory of languages long dead without a trace.
How, I wonder, did I become what I am not?

I request a break. The sounds cease.
I check the clock, calculate, write
figures in a notebook. I am numb
and stiff, walk up and down the hall,
stare into busy offices. I wait.

I wait for something forgotten, something
caught and bruised: a brown feather,
a shaft of green light, a certain word.
I bend, drink water, remember stubborn
clams clinging to the muddy bottom.

II.

The building across the street
has an ordinary facade, a view of the park
and rows of symmetrical spotless windows.
Each morning, the working women come to perform
their duties. They are in starched white,
could pass for vigilant nurses keeping
order and quiet around those about to die.
And each morning, idle women
in pale blue housecoats, frilled and fluffed
at the edges, stare out of double windows,
waiting for something to begin.

With whom would you change places, I ask
myself, the maid or the mistress?

III.

The clock sucks me back. I calculate the loss,
return to the books, his unrecognizing eyes.
He is unaware of the pantomime outside,
feels no rage that I and the world are lost
to him, only mourns the words dead on the page.
We begin again. I point to the paragraph,
synchronize the movement of eye and mouth,
abandon all pretense of feeling. Silently I float
out, out toward the horizon, out toward the open sea,
leaving behind the dull drone of an efficient machine.

I am
there again, standing by the railing, watching
the whales in their narrow aquarium, watching
their gleaming grace in the monotonous circle, watching
how they hunger for fleshly contact, how the young keeper
places his human hand in their rough pink mouths,
rubs their tongues, splashes them like babies. I cannot
watch them enough, but feel deeply ashamed for I know
the price.

With a shock I realize we are not together,
that he is lost, caught in a trap.
He sounds the words over and over, moves
the glass back and forth, insists there is
a lapse in meaning. I sit silent, tense, watch
as he painfully untangles the subtle error, watch
as he leans back exhausted saying: "I knew something
was wrong! I knew from the context that something
was wrong!"

IV.

At the end of the day I stack the galleys,
mark an *x* where we've been forced to stop.
He is reluctant to let me go, anxious, un-
certain about the coming days, but I smile,
assure him they'll be all the same. Alone,
I rush for the bulb-lit train, for the empty
corner of the dingy car, then begin the struggle
against his vacant stare, against the memory
of the crowded shelves.

It is a story, I tell myself, at least
a story, that one Sunday when I refused
to go to work. Fifteen, bored with inventory
and weekend jobs, I stayed in bed and,
already expert, called in sick. Her rage
was almost savage, wild. She paced
through the apartment, returned to me again
and again saying *"Get up! Get up now!"*
as if I were in mortal danger. But nothing
would move me from my bed, from the sun
cutting through the iron fire escape outside,
from the half-finished book about the man
and the whale. "It's not that much money,"
I called to her.

And then her inexplicable silence. At first
she sat in the kitchen, fingering the piece
of cloth, staring absently at the teacup.
Finally she got up, began pinning the pattern.
Soon I heard the clean sound of the scissor
against the kitchen table, then silence again
as she basted. Much later that day, she worked
on the machine, and still she did not speak
to me, just let the bobbing needle make its own
uninterrupted noise. And as I went to bed
new with the excitement of that sea of words,
filled with my own infinite possibilities, she
continued sewing, fulfilling her obligation
for the next day's fitting.

V.

The blind man balances easily in the rocking
car. He moves among us, sings, shakes a tin
cup. Most of us think it's all a con, but it
makes no difference. Pose is part of necessity.
Riding each evening through the echoing tunnels,
I've begun to believe in the existence of my own
soul, its frailty, its ability to grow narrow,
small. I've begun to understand what it means
to be born mute, to be born without hope of speech.

Work Sonnets
with Notes and a Monologue

I: Work Sonnets

i.

iceberg
I dream   yearning
to be fluid.
through how many nights
must it float   cumbersome
for how many centuries
of sun   how many
thousands of years
must it wait
so that one morning
I'll wake
as water of lake
of ocean
of the drinking well?

and day breaks.

ii.

today was another day. first i typed some
letters that had to get out. then i spent
hours xeroxing page after page after page
till it seemed that i was part of the machine
or that it was a living thing like me. its
blinking lights   its opening mouth   looked
as if they belonged to some kind of terrible
unthinking beast to whom i would always be bound.
oblivious to my existence   it simply waited
for its due   waited for me to keep it going
waited for me to provide page after page after page.
when it overheated   i had to stop while it
readied itself to receive again. so i typed
some letters that had to get out. and he said

he was pleased with the way things were going.

iii.

today was my day for feeling bitter. the xerox
broke down completely   and the receptionist
put her foot down   and made it clear to the repairmen
that *we* couldn't afford to keep such a machine
and it was costing *us* extra money everytime *we* had
to xerox outside. they hemmed and hawed and said
the fuzz from the carpet clogged things up   and
then they worked on it. and she watched over them
and made sure it was going properly when they left.
by then i'd fallen behind and he asked me to stay
late   and i said i was tired and really wanted to go
home. so he said it was really important and i could
come in late tomorrow with pay. so i said okay and
stayed. but i didn't feel any better about it.

a morning is not an evening.

iv.

volcano
I dream   yearning
to explode.
for how many centuries
of earth   relentless
grinding   how many
thousands of unchanged
years   buried
will it take
so that one morning
I'll wake
as unfettered flame
as liquid rock
as fertile ash?

and day breaks.

v.

today was my day for taking things in stride.
i was helpful to the temp in the office next
door   who seemed bewildered and who had definitely
lied about her skills. the dictaphone was
a mystery to her and she did not know how to use
the self-erasing IBM nor the special squeezer
to squeeze in words. she was the artist type:
hair all over the place   and dirty fingernails.
i explained everything to her   during her coffee
break   when she had deep creases in her forehead.
i felt on top of things. during lunch
i went out and walked around window shopping
feeling nice in the afternoon sun. and then
i returned and crashed through a whole bunch

of letters so i wouldn't have to stay late.

vi.

today was my day for feeling envy. i envied
every person who did not have to do what i
had to do. i envied every person who was rich
or even had 25 cents more than me   or worked
even one hour less. i envied every person who
had a different job   even though i didn't want
any of them either. i envied poor homeless children
wandering the streets because they were little
and didn't know the difference   or so i told myself.
and i envied the receptionist who'd been there
for years and years and years and is going to retire
soon   her hearing impaired from the headpiece she'd
once been forced to wear. For her it was over.
She was getting out. i envied her so much today.

i wanted to be old.

vii.

rock
I dream   yearning
to yield.
how many centuries
of water pounding
for how many thousands
of years   will it take
to erode this hardness
so that one morning
I'll wake
as soil
as moist clay
as pleasure sand
along the ocean's edge?

and day breaks.

viii.

today we had a party. he said he had gotten a
new title and brought in a bottle of wine during
lunch and we all sat around and joked about how
we'd become such important people and drank the
wine. and the receptionist got a little giddy
and they told her to watch it or she would develop
a terrible reputation which was not appropriate for
someone her age and maturity. and she laughed and
said "that's all right. i'll risk it." and the temp
from the office next door came in to ask me to go to
lunch. so we gave her some wine and she said she'd
been hired permanently and was real happy because
she'd been strung out and getting pretty desperate.
i noticed her hair was tied back and her nails neater.

and then we all got high and he said to everyone
this was a hell of a place. and then he announced
he had a surprise for me. he said he was going to
get a new xerox because it was a waste of my time to
be doing that kind of work and he had more important
things for me to do. and everyone applauded and the
receptionist said she hoped this one was better than
the last because we sure were losing money on that
old clinker. and he assured her it was. and then he
welcomed the temp to the floor and said "welcome aboard."
and he told her across the hall they treat their people
like we treat our people and their place is one hell
of a place to work in as she'd soon discover. and then
he winked over in my direction and said: "ask her.

she knows all about it."

ix.

dust
I dream   yearning
to form.
through how much emptiness
must it speed
for how many centuries
of aimless orbits
how many thousands
of light years   must it wait
so that one morning
I'll wake
as cratered moon
as sea-drenched planet
as exploding sun?

and day breaks.

and day breaks.

II: Notes

Says she's been doing this for 12 years. Her fifth job since she started working at 18. The others were: office of paperbox manufacturing co. (cold and damp almost all year round); office of dress factory (was told she could also model for buyers; quit because buyers wanted to feel the materials and her; was refused a reference); office of make-up distributor (got discounts on products); real estate office; and this, which she considers the best one. Through high school, she worked part-time contributing towards household expenses.

Extremely sharp with them. Says: "I'm not a tape recorder. Go through that list again." Or: "It's impossible. I've got too much to do." Two days ago, she told me: "Make *them* set the priorities. Don't make yourself nuts. You're not a machine."

Am surprised, because I always feel intimidated. But she seems instinctively to understand power struggles. Is able to walk the fine line between doing her job well and not knocking herself out beyond what she thinks she is being paid for. And she *is* good. Quick. Extremely accurate. Am always embarrassed when they return things with errors and ask me to do them over again. Never happens to her. She's almost always letter perfect.

I've told her she should demand more. The dictaphone is old and the typewriter is always breaking down. She should make them get her better equipment. It's too frustrating the way it is. She shrugged. Said it really didn't matter to her. Was surprised at her indifference.

Friendly, yet somehow distant. Sometimes I think she's suspicious of me, though I've tried to play down my background. I've said to her: "What's the difference? We're doing exactly the same work, aren't we?" Did not respond. Yet, whenever I've had trouble, she's always been ready to help.

Her inner life: an enigma. Have no idea what preoccupies her. Would be interested in knowing her dreams. Hard for me to imagine. This is a real problem. 1st person demands such inside knowledge, seems really risky. Am unclear what the overall view would be. What kind of vision presented. How she sees the world. How she sees herself in it. It seems all so limited, so narrow. 3rd person opens it up. But it would be too distanced, I think. I want to be inside her. Make the reader feel what she feels. A real dilemma. I feel so outside.

Says she reads, but is never specific what. Likes music, dancing. Smokes. Parties a lot, I think, for she seems tired in the morning and frequently says she did not get much sleep. Lives by herself. Thinks she should get married, but somehow can't bring herself to do it. "I like having the place to myself," she said the other day. Didn't specify what she was protecting.

Attitude towards them remains also unformulated. Never theorizes or distances herself from her experience. She simply responds to the immediate situation. Won't hear of organizing which she considers irrelevant (and also foreign inspired). Yet she's very, very fair and helpful to others and always indignant if someone is being treated unfairly. Whenever a temp arrives, she always shows her what's what. Tells her not to knock herself out. Reminds her to take her coffee break. Once gave up her lunch hour so one of them could go to the dentist for a bad tooth. Did it without hesitation. For a stranger.

Q: Is she unique or representative? The final piece: an individual voice? or a collective one?

I've learned a lot here, I think. It hasn't been as much of a loss as I expected. At least I've gotten some ideas and some material. But thank god I'm leaving next week. Can't imagine spending a whole life doing this.

III: A Monologue about a Dialogue

And she kept saying: "There's more. Believe me, there's more."

And I was kind of surprised because I couldn't imagine what more there could be. And then I began to wonder what she meant by the more, like maybe a bigger apartment or more expensive restaurants.

But she said that wasn't it, not really. "I'm not materialistic," she said and then looked kind of hopeless, as if I could never understand her. "I just want to *do* something," she said, obviously frustrated. And she looked hopeless again. And then she took a big breath, as if she was going to make a real effort at explaining it to me.

"It's just," she said, "it makes no difference whether I'm here or not. *Anyone* can do this. And I've always wanted to do special, important work."

Well, that made me laugh, because I've stopped wanting to do any work at all. All work is bullshit. Everyone knows that. No matter how many telephones and extensions, no matter how many secretaries, no matter how many names in the rolodex. It's all bullshit.

But she disagreed. "No," she said. "There's really important work to be done."

"Like what?" I asked curious, for I've seen enough of these types running around telling me how important it is to do this or that and just because they're telling me it's important they start feeling that they're important and doing important work. So I was curious to see what she'd come up with.

But she was kind of vague, and said something about telling the truth and saying things other people refused to say. And I confess I'd never heard it put that way before.

"I want to be able to say things, to use words," she explained.

"Oh, a writer," I said. I suddenly understood.

"Well, yes. But not like you think. Not romances or anything like that. I want to write about you and how you work and how it should be better for you."

"So that's it," I said, understanding now even more than I had realized at first. "So that's the important work. That certainly sounds good. Good for you, that is. But what about me? Do you think there's more for me? Because I'm not about to become a writer. And I don't know why I should just keep doing this so you have something to write about that's important. So can you think of something more for me? I mean I can't do anything except this."

And I could feel myself getting really mad because I remembered how in school they kept saying: "Stop daydreaming and concentrate!" And they said that your fingertips had to memorize the letters so that it would feel as if they were part of the machine. And at first it seemed so strange, because everything was pulling me away, away from the machine. And I really wanted to think about what was going on outside. There seemed so many things, though I can't recall them now. But they kept pushing me and pushing me: "Stop daydreaming! Concentrate!" And finally I did. And after a while it didn't seem so hard to do. And I won first prize in class. And the teacher said I'd have a real good choice in the jobs I could get because quality is always appreciated in this world and with quality you can get by.

And when I remembered how I'd sat doing those exercises, making my fingertips memorize the letters, I was real mad because she was no different than the others. There's always something more. More for them. But not one notion about something more for me. Except maybe a better machine so that I can do more work more quickly. Or maybe a couple of hours less a week. That's the most that they can ever think of for me.

And I was so furious. I'd heard all this before. And I know that as soon as they tell you they'll fight to get you better working conditions, they go home and announce: "You couldn't pay me enough to do that kind of work." That's what they say behind your back.

And I started to yell at her: "If you got words and know what to say, how come you can't come up with something more for me?"

And she was so startled. I could see it in her eyes. I mean you've got to have nerve. I'm supposed to just stay here while she writes about me and my work.

And then I said: "They're always going to need people to type the final copies. And I can see you'll never waste your time with that once you've thought of all the right words." And she kind of backed up, because I must have looked really mad. And she bumped into the file cabinet and couldn't move back any further. And I said to her: "What's the difference to me? It's all the same. I always end up doing the same thing. So let's make it clear between us. Whenever you finish whatever it is you're writing about me and my work, don't count on me to help you out in the final stages. Never count on me, no matter how good the working conditions."

A Poem for Judy
beginning a new job

I will keep this simple
not give it
universal significance
nor transform it
into art.

You say:
"I will not do this
forever. I *will* paint."

I've learned now
that it's no solace
to point out   the others
so many others
straining   wasting
unable to do
what they know
they must do

for such loss
is always solitary
and unshared
outside the scope
of bloodless theory.

You do not paint
and what must happen
does not happen:
the transformation
on the empty canvas
of the elusive marble
into the shadowy water
or of the simple water
into impenetrable rock

and nothing
nothing
not even a loving embrace
nor special intimate
midnight talk
will ever make up

or diminish that loss
for you
or for her
or her
or her

or her.

III. Urban Flowers

Mnemonic Devices:
Brooklyn Botanic Gardens, 1981

1.

I'd forgotten. Despite the planters
blossoming in the northern light
despite the potted succulents
over which you take such care
and patience   despite the window boxes
wired to the crumbling ledges
I'd forgotten.

This morning   at the pond's edge   we watch
the energetic ducks   chase and fly
in enigmatic patterns. I declare it
a mating dance—an educated guess—
having lost the thread of cycles
seasons   time   except when April's
sharp insistent air   distracts us
from this city's bitter dream
and we rise one morning   and remember:

there are still the gardens.

2.

It is a ritual   for us
this annual return
to the unsuppressed spring
in this guarded landscape
to the flowers   and trees
earth   rocks   pond.

It is the stuff of mythology
both old and new   as we relive
once more   a certain day
suddenly grown   strange
and dim   and how we stood
uncertain and afraid
of the exploding lightning
and the silent trees.

That day   awakened in us images
long lost   amid the dangers
of the city streets   and
we stood amazed   at the sight
and sound   wondering
what else   we'd lost.

That day   the gardens
drenched in violent rains
were transformed   into a raw
uncultivated place. And we
were   wearied wanderers
dazed   in awe   having suddenly
stumbled into our native land.

Royal Pearl

Where do new varieties come from?

General Eisenhower is a red tulip which was first recog-
nized in 1951.

In 1957 a lemon yellow mutation appeared in a field
of red General Eisenhower tulips. This yellow mutation
proved to be a stable sport which was called—Royal Pearl.
—Brooklyn Botanic Gardens

In dead of winter   imprisoned within
the imprisoned earth   it was a leap
defiant   of all eternal laws   and patterns.
Beneath the frozen earth   it came to be
like a splitting of an inner will
a wrenching from a designated path
a sudden burst   from a cause unknown.
And then in spring   it opened: a lemon yellow
in a pure red field.

Our words deny the simple beauty
the wild energy of the event. *Anomaly*
deviant   mutant   we're always taught
as though this world   were a finished place
and we the dull guardians   of its perfected forms.
Our lives are rooted in such words.

Yet each winter   there are some
who watch   the gardens   emptied
only white   as the snow presses
on the fenced-in grounds   just
as on an unclaimed field.
And each winter   there are some
who dream   of a splitting of an inner will
a wrenching from the designated path
who dream a purple flower   standing solitary
in a yellow field.

Lithops

Common name: living stone

Barely differentiated
from the inorganic   they conceal
their passions   in sheer survival.
It is philosophy: life's hard
growth and erosion   even rocks
in the end   are broken down
to formless dust.

But like all schema   incomplete
for between the grey and fleshy
crevices   strange blossoms grow
in brazen colors. For us it is
the ancient sign   that every life
has its secret longings   to transcend
the daily pressing need
longings   that one day   must flower.

Aesthetics

No beauty for beauty's sake here.
Life's too lean
a constant   "Let's get down
to brass tacks." Function and necessity.
Stone and water.

Like the popularity of narcissus bulbs
this season. Not as you'd expect
for the plant itself   which sprouts
endless green stalks   that rise up
stiff and straight   and then finally
eke out a few buds of puny white flowers.
Nor for the obvious lesson by example:
the unavoidable six weeks (maybe more)
of patient preparation   before
any real prospects of blooming.

But rather   for the roots beneath.
Brown tipped and firm   they probe
and press around the artificial stones
in intricate networks   even dead-end mazes
daring anyone to trace them back
to their original source. In the stores
the saleswomen warn: "They can toss
the stones right out of the container!"
And here   that remains the real attraction.

Winter Light

Almost December. Indifferent
to seasons   the marigolds
persist. I am surprised by their pluck
and lack of propriety
their ability to ignore
the inappropriate:
a rusted leaking window box
a shaky fire escape
leading to a cemented street
below. They do not mourn
that all good things must
come to an end   and accept
that end as fate or destiny.
Instead   without struggle
or assessment of soil
moisture   heat   air   they continue
blooming   in chilling winter light
exactly as they did all summer.

Oleander

A gift from a lover when things
were definitely   going downhill.
"It's poisonous," she said.
"No known antidotes."
After the breakup   long after
when I'd already settled down
with someone else   I boarded it
with my mother   who's always taught:
never throw anything out.

Whenever I see it   I am drawn again
to the sembling innocence   among the dark
green jade and purple passion. I long
to taste one leaf   one petal   to test
that warning   for nothing   I tell myself
not even death   could be that final.
You must understand   it is more
than mortal resistance
for there was a time   when she left
and I knew   was fiercely certain
this departure   was the last.

Cactus

for my mother
Rose Perczykow Klepfisz

The pot itself was half the story.
A yellow ceramic dime store knickknack
of a featureless Mexican
with a large sombrero   pushing a wagon
filled with dirt.

The cactus was the other half.
Self-effacing   it didn't demand much
which was just as well
since she had no spare time
for delicate cultivation.
Used to just the bare essentials
it stood on our kitchen windowsill
two floors above the inhospitable soil
and neither flourished   grew
nor died.

I'd catch her eyeing it
as she stood   breathless
broiling our dinner's minute steaks
her profile centered in the windowframe.
She understood   the meaning   of both pot
and plant   still would insist there was
something extra   the colors yellow
green   or as she once explained
in her stiff   night school English:
"It is always   of importance to see
the things aesthetical."

Abutilon in Bloom

for Diana Bellessi

Abutilon: flowering indoor maple; houseplant

Cultivated inside   out of the bounds
of nature   it stubborned
on the windowsill   six winters and springs
resisting water   sun   all researched care.
It would not give   beyond its leaves.

Yet today   in the morning light
the sudden color asserts itself
among the spotted green   and I
pause   before another empty day
and wonder at its wild blooming.

It leans against the sunwarm glass
its blossoms firm on the thick stems
as if its roots
absorbed the knowledge
that there is no other place
that memory is only pain
that even here   now
we must burst forth with orange flowers
with savage hues of our captivity.

IV. Inhospitable Soil

i can't go back
where i came from was
burned off the map

i'm a jew
anywhere is someone else's land

—Melanie Kaye

Glimpses of the Outside

in memory of
Marcia Tillotson (1940-1981)

A place

1.

Cherry Plain was once called South Berlin   before
the war   and then they probably became self-conscious.
Many here   go back before the Revolution   are of
Hessian descent   fought with the British. They are
wary of strangers   defined as anyone who has not lived
here since birth. Still they chat politely   wave
as I drive by. The children are more open   stare
shamelessly   at the new woman in town. It is a quiet
place. One post office. One small general store.
It could have grown and developed   when they expanded
old route 22. But it would have meant   cutting into
the cemetery   and of course   that was out of the question.
Like disgruntled children   they protest over their parents'
limitations   for they see   they could have gotten something
off the weekenders   rushing back and forth on Friday
and Sunday nights. But ancestors will have their way.
So 22 looped around it   leaving the town intact   except
for the occasional stranger   who is looking for a way out.

2.

I have decided not to plant a garden   only to scavenge.
Already last year's furrows   (the result of others'
labor)   are vague   and the borders almost completely
obscured by the undisciplined   self-absorbed growth.
It is what we know of weeds: no delicate sense of
intrusion   of transgressing bounds. They move in
take over   and that's that. It doesn't bother me
this unreflecting rudeness. I am satisfied to witness
the few carrot sprigs   onions   tiny lettuce heads
and without commitment   to clear weedless islands
around them. The asparagus reaches its full growth

merges with the stalk   and goes to seed. The delicate
dill   follows suit   achieves its natural toughness.
I do not intercede   in these events.

3.

This house was once a meeting hall   then a dance
hall   a polling place. More recently   a garage.
I want to plant flowers around its edges   bring
to life an image   I have had about it. But the
earth is naturally tough with rocks   and more   it
is clogged with rusted screws and washers   sparkplugs
colored chips of glass   all conspiring against my
trowel. Then too there is the heavy oil   already
congealed   fixed and unyielding   like ancient geological
strata. The inner image long forgotten   I tense
against this human resistance   push harder towards
an earlier time   towards less polluted soil.

4.

I have started transplanting wild flowers   whose
names I do not know. Small blue ones from a lake
in a state park. They are modest   with pale yellow
centers   used to the moisture of the water's edge.
I douse them every morning to make them feel at home.
From a roadside   I dig out bright yellow ones   plant
them by the unpainted barn   so I can see them from my
window as I work. These thrive   as if their sole pur-
pose   was my pleasure. But exotic   tall purple flowers
with bulb-type roots   strong like twine in their tie
to the earth   and to their particular spot   these shrivel
up a few hours after being placed by the barn. I consider
the possibilities: individual will   personality   simple
biochemical make-up. Whatever. These do not adapt.
They stand tall   and elegant   dried by the sun   next to
the brilliant yellow flowers   for whom a place by the barn
is as good   as a roadbank.

5.

Midnight: the meadow is sparkling with fireflies.
I had always thought   that at night   they folded their
wings   over their iridescent bodies   and darkened
that light. Yet here they are   in constant motion
lighting against the shadow of the mountain. The
memory suddenly comes alive   like the underside of
a non-living stone. I am eight years old   and it is
almost dusk. The fireflies rush   through arid city
air. I trap them in a milk bottle   hoping to create
a lantern to light my way home. I do not understand
that not even the dusty grass   hurriedly pressed through
the narrow bottleneck   will keep them alive   that
inevitably   in such confinement (is it a lack of air
or simply a lack of space for flight?)   their light will
dim and die.

6.

What could go wrong in such a setting? I ask
myself   thinking of that arid air   left behind
of the wino sleeping in my doorway   every night.
This valley   is so quiet   so clear and sharp-
edged   in the summer daylight. The old houses
meticulously painted   and the lawns carefully mowed
declare only: order and plain living. What could
go wrong in such a setting? I ask myself again.
The mountains look permanent   eternal in fact
though all I read about human life   about natural
evolution   tells me everything is in constant
motion   that this landscape was once of a different
sort   that these people who distrust strangers
were once strangers themselves   that the sign
"Indian Massacre Road"   a sign indistinguishable
from any other in lettering and color   posted modestly
at an obscure crossing   is but a barely noticeable
vestige   of one history forgotten and unattended.

7.

The pump is old   its age reflected in its weight
iron   shaped and welded more than a half a century ago.
It draws the water noisily   slowly   sounding like
a failing heart   pounding against itself. The plumbers
cluck their tongues   in masculine admiration. "She's
a goddam antique"   the young one says. He is tall
and handsome   with clear blue eyes. "Don't make those
anymore"   he continues   with a voice of experience
his age denies. I suspect he's only an apprentice   for
he descends into the well   while the older man sits
casually on the ledge   occasionally offering advice.
They're in agreement   or in cahoots. Get a new pump.
This one's definitely shot. Not worth fixing   the parts
too difficult to find   and when found   too expensive.
I decide against it   at least for now   and tell them
to see if anything can be done. Later   I return and
ask   if they can patch it up. "Sure"   the young one
answers. "I'll take anything on   as long as it's white."

A visit

1.

The woman who is coming to visit   is my mother.
Her life   has been bracketed by historical events
over which she's had no control. During World War II
she developed a canniness for detecting Jews   did
not care how many documents they had to prove   who
they were not. She knew. She could tell   by a special
look in their eyes   a gesture of the hand   a confidence
too casual. This acquired ability   so finely tuned
during the war years   remains alive   so that today
decades later   she cannot wander far from her Jewish
neighborhood   before she begins assessing   who are
the safe ones   and who are not.

2.

Her survival   (and as a result mine)   was partly
dependent on: her small nose   her grey eyes. And
most critical: her impeccable Polish   (with no trace
of a Yiddish accent)   because an older sister had
insisted she attend Polish schools   to gain greater
mobility. It was one perspective on the Jewish condition
in Poland. At critical moments   these elements   heredity
and environment   combined in the right proportions to
create luck. But there was also another   character
or in this case   guts. When the Germans came for her
she begged: *Ich habe ein kleines kind.* And when she
saw   the sliver of hesitation in their eyes   she ran
and took her chances. They did not chase   or shoot
just let her go. For months   she convinced the peasants
she was a Pole   playing a part   ad-libbing the dialogue
without a flaw   pretending to be the human being   they
assumed she was. During this time   she learned survival
depends on complete distrust. Even today   she is still
fierce   in her refusal to rely on others. Some would call
it alienation. Others pride. I think   it's only
the necessary stance   of any survivor.

3.

History   she says with irony   has a way of repeating
itself. *Then*   she outwitted two German soldiers   probably
young men   taught from childhood   the hideousness of
Jews. Faced with a woman   fair and ordinary   pleading
for her sickly child who would be orphaned   they must have
thought: No   this cannot be that Jewish monster. And
she escaped. At least momentarily. *Now*   she is trapped
again. But no walls or barbed wire   around her this time.
No plans for uprisings   or secret meetings. Each evening
she returns   hurrying through the orderly streets   ominous
in their emptiness   and steps into the elevator. I want
to offer her advice   strategy   a philosophy   but know their
utter uselessness in this age. For *now*   is a vastly
different time and place. The country is not occupied
by strangers. Those she fears most   are not an enemy.
And neglect and hunger   cannot be outwitted.

4.

We visit the Hancock Shaker Village   walking through
the restored buildings   recreated workrooms and living
quarters. I note the quietness   the simplicity of
the line   and wonder about the eye that fashioned it
the aesthetic vision   the philosophy of light   air
of raising the struggle for survival   above humiliation.
We pass through the herb garden. My mother stops
looks in amazement at the round stone barn   and marvels
how all this could have come   to a dead stop   without
catastrophe   without disaster. She scrutinizes the
photographs of children   adopted and nurtured. "How
could they not have wanted children of their own?"
she asks   having always believed   that one's own blood is
the sole source   of all security. And I see her shift
as she tells me again   of the children   hidden in convents
baptised and converted   then claimed by relatives after
the war. Many were finally kidnapped   or their protectors
bribed and bought off. Some could never be reclaimed.
For those who were   it was hard   painful   but my mother
adds   "They were our only hope."

5.

But it is not simply a question of reproduction
I tell myself that night   thinking of my own child-
lessness. They lacked something   which would have
pushed them on   which would have given them   a hook
in time. But it was time itself   that they ignored
thinking the farmland and woods   around the village
the seasons emerging predictably   in full character
the day and the night   all these   they assumed were
heaven   eternal. At the end of each day   after baking
and laundry   welding and weaving   tending the children
and the fields   they would meet   and reaffirm their faith.
First they shook out the sins from their bodies   then
danced holding their palms up   to gather in the blessings.
There was no time   there was no death. And so they
lived   and so they died.

6.

My mother boards the train   and sits behind the
tinted glass. She mouths words and gestures   nothing
I can understand. I raise my arms in frustration
motion her to try again. She does   but the barriers
remain. She writes a note   on a piece of paper   holds
it against the glass. The European script is clear:
"It is empty here. It is cool." I smile   and give
the okay sign. She will be comfortable on her trip back
to the city. Still   I am all anxiety. Departures
swell old   undefined fears in me   the fear of permanent
separations. Old   long-forgotten departures   which
remain active in me   like instinct. The fear of being
lost and never found   of losing all trace   all connections
severed   the thread broken. (When after two years   she
came to get me from the orphanage   I cried when I caught
sight of her   and raised my arms to her. I was barely
three   but I had not forgotten.) Of endless   futile
searches for relatives long vanished   or even worse
alive   but not traceable.

The train begins to move. My mother sits behind the tinted glass and waves. Her face becomes an angle   and then disappears. Her words were: "Find a place where you are happy." But the sound of those words   had the mourning of separation.

A place in time

1.

The postmistress is insecure in her calculations.
She checks   and rechecks all her figures   never having
the ease of certainty. Still   I trust her view
of this place   for she has that tutored eye   able to
detect the changes   nuances and variations   whose
implications   remain obscure to my alien reasoning.
She is chatty   inquisitive. Sometimes   I think she must
be lonely   sitting all day by herself   behind the old-
fashioned post office boxes   decorated with elaborate
brass eagles. Perhaps the grocery will be sold (and then
we'll be stuck   with whoever buys it). Perhaps the mail
truck   will be traded in   (and then we'll have regular
delivery). Perhaps the church will be painted   by early
fall (and we can begin having services again). Perhaps
the rumors about the metal barrels   buried in the nearby
camp grounds are true   (and we should stop swimming
in that lake).

2.

At first   the cats were cautious   flattening
themselves   along the ground   slinking close to
the edges of the house. No vestigial recollections
springing from the unconscious depth of the species.
Or so I thought. But now   and I can hardly measure
the time elapsed   they act as if it's all they've
ever known   routinely bringing in mice from the meadow
or bodies of birds   necks snapped   heads hanging
like colored limp sacks. I glimpse my favorite
the tortoise shell   eating a rabbit   whose belly seems
expertly slashed and exposed. She hunches   over it
calmly chewing   the juicy red meat   patiently breaking
through   the sinewy flesh.

3.

At the Burr & Grille in Averill Park   only men
are at the bar. They look like mechanics: oil
streaked pants   workgloves stuffed in pockets.
They swap army stories   their glimpses of the
outside. In Haiti   I overhear   there are only
the rich and the poor. "Nothing in the middle"
a man in his twenties says. The rich live on top
of the mountain   the poor by the sea. They earn
about $35 a year. "Imagine the kind of life   *that*
is. They're starving. Imagine! In this day and age!"
Burr   behind the bar   clucks his tongue. "In China"
he says   "they fight over candybars. Imagine what
that must be like." The young one begins again:
"You know   you get off   and they have all those
bands and colorful costumes   and everything is all
welcome. And then you take five steps away from
the pier   and *wham*! [he bangs his hand down on the bar]
they're ready to slit your throat   to get that wallet!"

4.

Saturday: The Baptist Church flea market and auction
offers the predictable merchandise. Old clothes
battered pots and pans   chipped glassware   rusted lawn
furniture. "It's all for a good cause"   a woman tells
me   and mentions interior renovations. I wonder if I'm
the only Jew in the crowd. An older man approaches.
"Smile!" he orders. "The Lord loves you! Certainly
the Lord loves you!" I nod   feel uncomfortable   move
towards another table. A woman   about seven months
pregnant   is having her purchases priced. She is no
more than twenty   with a small pale face   faintly freckled
deeply worn. Dressed in colorless bermudas   and a gray
blouse   she holds a carton of baby clothes. On the ground
by her feet are cheap games of plastic   a round container
with broken wooden logs   the debris of an old erector set.
This too   is her collection   the necessary response
to life's gnawing insistence on itself   on not being

ignored. She looks wearied   almost emptied by her vigilance.
I watch as she hands over the ten dollar bill and waits
for the change   watch   as she smiles   and turns away.

5.

I ride the backroads   far from any village or town
far from the blacktops   carefully numbered. Woods
along both sides. Suddenly   I am startled by an
unexpected home   a trailer on a small patch of cleared
land. Logic would say   that it had no stability
the cinderblocks at its corners appearing flimsy   unable
to keep it firmly rooted to the ground. Yet the faded
paint   the obvious rust creeping along its outer shell
reveal a hard-won permanence. Barefoot children stop
playing in front of a torn screen door   stand anxious
tentative   waiting for the unfamiliar car to pass.
A woman's eyes   keep guard at a kitchen window. Plastic
deer and clay ducks line the worn path. Junked cars
spill out of the collapsed garage. Gray overalls   and
bright sheets with sunsets   dry between two shade trees.
In a carved out tractor tire   painted red and white   grow
yellow marigolds   blue petunias. An orderly vegetable
garden on one side   loose piles of freshly split logs
on the other   testify to the implacable needs of winter.
All is urgency   asymmetry in this territory resistant
to maps and philosophy. Only the seasons   and birth
and death   remain stark. I know   I see   I learn again
from the anxiety in that woman's eyes   in the caution
of the children's stance   that there is no escape.

Mourning

1.

I reread his letter. He writes about your struggle
Marcia   your will to survive. I read the letter again
and stare at the mountain's outline   behind the house.
It is will   against the dark shadowy mountain   that I
keep thinking about. How you refused   up to the last
moment   refused to say   it is over   but stretched out
your time   how you were willing to endure the pain   how
you would not be separated from it   because it alone
held the possibility of life. A few days before you died
a friend said: *Everything's collapsing   but she simply
refuses.* I think about that refusal to cooperate   to give
yourself an easeful death. It is your will   Marcia
I am trying to understand.

2.

Why so hard to absorb   after all the waiting?
The daily calls   and reports   turned your body
into a machine. The nurses were polite   precise.
Respiratory arrest. Cardiac failure. She's
breathing on her own now. Somewhat better.
"How is her spirit?" I ask stupidly   as if
the answer could make a bond between us. One
time they said: She is angry.   Another: She is
somewhat anxious.

3.

Death asserts itself as everywhere   pulls me out
of the eternal   roots me in this time   in this place.
Your death   Marcia. After thirteen years of struggles
who would have thought   this was the final one   who
would have thought   this one was different   from all
the others? It is something I must plant   I keep saying
as if I could contain the loss   by finding the right
piece of ground   by the barn perhaps   or by the gigantic

ash   that hovers over the house   a tree planted by
a neighbor's father   more than sixty years ago. I
need a place for your death   Marcia   for it feels like
an emptiness   that can erode   all the mountains
that protect this valley.

4.

But there is no possibility of containing it. All
the days merge   and only hindsight   reveals the subtle
but discrete changes: the shortened daylight
the slowly   yellowing grass. I place seeds in the bird
feeder   write letters home   check the final stages of
the garden's undisciplined growth. Everything is
shrivelling   emptying itself of body and substance
huddling closer and closer to the earth. I plant bulbs
like a skeptic   never fully believing   these drab
lifeless lumps   will bloom next year   in full exotic color.
Nothing   I think   staring at the sixty-year-old ash
should be taken for granted. I push my trowel   deeper
sift out the slivers of glass   the heavy nails   place
the bulbs in their designated places   then cover them
with soil   flattening the surface with my hand.

Bashert

These words are dedicated to those who died

These words are dedicated to those who died
because they had no love and felt alone in the world
because they were afraid to be alone and tried to stick it out
because they could not ask
because they were shunned
because they were sick and their bodies could not resist the
disease
because they played it safe
because they had no connections
because they had no faith
because they felt they did not belong and wanted to die

These words are dedicated to those who died
because they were loners and liked it
because they acquired friends and drew others to them
because they took risks
because they were stubborn and refused to give up
because they asked for too much

These words are dedicated to those who died
because a card was lost and a number was skipped
because a bed was denied
because a place was filled and no other place was left

These words are dedicated to those who died
because someone did not follow through
because someone was overworked and forgot
because someone left everything to God
because someone was late
because someone did not arrive at all
because someone told them to wait and they just couldn't any
longer

These words are dedicated to those who died
because death is a punishment
because death is a reward

ba-shert (Yiddish): inevitable, (pre)destined.

because death is the final rest
because death is eternal rage

These words are dedicated to those who died

Bashert

These words are dedicated to those who survived

These words are dedicated to those who survived
because their second grade teacher gave them books
because they did not draw attention to themselves and got lost
in the shuffle
because they knew someone who knew someone else who could
help them and bumped into them on a corner on a Thursday
afternoon
because they played it safe
because they were lucky

These words are dedicated to those who survived
because they knew how to cut corners
because they drew attention to themselves and always got picked
because they took risks
because they had no principles and were hard

These words are dedicated to those who survived
because they refused to give up and defied statistics
because they had faith and trusted in God
because they expected the worst and were always prepared
because they were angry
because they could ask
because they mooched off others and saved their strength
because they endured humiliation
because they turned the other cheek
because they looked the other way

These words are dedicated to those who survived
because life is a wilderness and they were savage
because life is an awakening and they were alert
because life is a flowering and they blossomed
because life is a struggle and they struggled
because life is a gift and they were free to accept it

These words are dedicated to those who survived

Bashert

1. Poland, 1944: My mother is walking down a road.

My mother is walking down a road. Somewhere in Poland. Walking towards an unnamed town for some kind of permit. She is carrying her Aryan identity papers. She has left me with an old peasant who is willing to say she is my grandmother.

She is walking down a road. Her terror in leaving me behind, in risking the separation is swallowed now, like all other feelings. But as she walks, she pictures me waving from the dusty yard, imagines herself suddenly picked up, the identity papers challenged. And even if she were to survive that, would she ever find me later? She tastes the terror in her mouth again. She swallows.

I am over three years old, corn silk blond and blue eyed like any Polish child. There is terrible suffering among the peasants. Starvation. And like so many others, I am ill. Perhaps dying. I have bad lungs. Fever. An ugly ear infection that oozes pus. None of these symptoms are disappearing.

The night before, my mother feeds me watery soup and then sits and listens while I say my prayers to the Holy Mother, Mother of God. I ask her, just as the nuns taught me, to help us all: me, my mother, the old woman. And then catching myself, learning to use memory, I ask the Mother of God to help my father. The Polish words slip easily from my lips. My mother is satisfied. The peasant has perhaps heard and is reassured. My mother has found her to be kind, but knows that she is suspicious of strangers.

My mother is sick. Goiter. Malnutrition. Vitamin deficiencies. She has skin sores which she cannot cure. For months now she has been living in complete isolation, with no point of reference outside of herself. She has been her own sole advisor, companion, comforter. Almost everyone of her world is dead: three sisters, nephews and nieces, her mother, her husband, her in-laws. All gone. Even the remnants of the resistance, those few left after the uprising, have dispersed into the Polish countryside. She is more alone than she could have ever imagined. Only she knows her real name and she is perhaps dying. She is thirty years old.

I am over three years old. I have no consciousness of our danger, our separateness from the others. I have no awareness that we are playing a part. I only know that I have a special name, that I have been named for the Goddess of Peace. And each night, I sleep secure in that knowledge. And when I wet my bed, my mother places me on her belly and lies on the stain. She fears the old woman and hopes her body's warmth will dry the sheet before dawn.

My mother is walking down a road. Another woman joins her. My mother sees through the deception, but she has promised herself that never, under any circumstances, will she take that risk. So she swallows her hunger for contact and trust and instead talks about the sick child left behind and lies about the husband in the labor camp.

Someone is walking towards them. A large, strange woman with wild red hair. They try not to look at her too closely, to seem overly curious. But as they pass her, my mother feels something move inside her. The movement grows and grows till it is an explosion of yearning that she cannot contain. She stops, orders her companion to continue without her. And then she turns.

The woman with the red hair has also stopped and turned. She is grotesque, bloated with hunger, almost savage in her rags. She and my mother move towards each other. Cautiously, deliberately, they probe past the hunger, the swollen flesh, the infected skin, the rags. Slowly, they begin to pierce five years of encrusted history. And slowly, there is perception and recognition.

In this wilderness of occupied Poland, in this vast emptiness where no one can be trusted, my mother has suddenly, bizarrely, met one of my father's teachers. A family friend. Another Jew.

They do not cry, but weep as they chronicle the dead and count the living. Then they rush to me. To the woman I am a familiar sight. She calculates that I will not live out the week, but comments only on my striking resemblance to my father. She says she has contacts. She leaves. One night a package of food is delivered anonymously. We eat. We begin to bridge the gap towards life. We survive.

2. Chicago, 1964: I am walking home alone at midnight.

I am walking home alone at midnight. I am a student of literature, and each night I stay in the library until it closes. Yet each night, as I return I still feel unprepared for the next day. The nature of literary movements eludes me. I only understand individual writers. I have trouble remembering genre definitions, historical dates and names, cannot grasp their meaning, significance. A whole world of abstractions and theories remains beyond my reach, on the other side of a wall I cannot climb over.

So each night, I walk home clutching my books as if I were a small school child. The city is alien. Since coming to America, this is my first time away from a Jewish neighborhood, Jewish friends, and I feel isolated, baffled at how to make a place for myself in this larger, gentile world which I have entered.

I am walking home alone at midnight. The university seems an island ungrounded. Most of its surrounding streets have been emptied. On some, all evidence of previous life removed except for occasional fringes of rubble that reveal vague outlines that hint at things that were. On others, old buildings still stand, though these are hollow like caves, once of use and then abandoned. Everything is poised. Everything is waiting for the emptiness to close in upon itself, for the emptiness to be filled up, for the emptiness to be swallowed and forgotten.

Walking home, I am only dimly aware of the meaning of this strange void through which I pass. I am even less aware of the dangers for someone like me, a woman walking home alone at midnight. I am totally preoccupied with another time, another place. Night after night, protected by the darkness, I think only of Elza who is dead. I am trying to place a fact about her, a fact which stubbornly resists classification: nothing that happened to her afterwards mattered. All that agonized effort. All that caring. *None of that mattered!*

At the end of the war, friends come to claim her. With the cold, calculated cunning of an adult, the eight year old vehemently denies who she is. No she is not who they think. Not a Jew. They have made a mistake. Mixed her up with another Elza. This one belongs here, with her mother.

She is simply being scrupulous in following her parents' instructions. "Do not ever admit to anyone who you are. It is our secret. Eventually we will come for you. Remember! *Never admit who you are!* Promise!"

Four years later, the war is over. Her parents dead. She is still bound by her promise. This woman *is* her mother. Her parents' friends know better. The woman has been kind, has saved her. But she is a Pole and Elza is a Jew. Finally, the bribe is big enough and the child released. Elza becomes an orphan.

And afterwards? She is adopted and finally seems to have everything. Two parents. Two handsome brothers. A house. Her own room. She studies Latin and does translations. Is valedictorian of her class. Goes away to college. Has boyfriends, affairs. Comes to New York. Works. Begins graduate school. Explicates Dylan Thomas, T. S. Eliot. Marries.

But none of it matters. She cannot keep up. The signs are clear. She is a poor housekeeper. Insists they eat off paper plates. She buys enough clothes to fill all her closets. But nothing soothes her. Finally she signs her own papers. Is released within a few months. I finish college and leave for Europe. Three weeks later, she checks into a hotel and takes an overdose. She is twenty-five years old.

Fearing I too might be in danger, my mother instructs Polish Jews resettled in Paris and Tel Aviv: "Don't tell her!" And to me she writes: "Elza is in the hospital again. There is no hope." I am suspicious, refer to her whenever I can. I am alert. Sense a discomfort, an edge I cannot define. I think I know, but I never dare ask. I come home. Seven months after her death, I finally know.

A story she once told me remains alive. During the war, the Polish woman sends her to buy a notebook for school. She is given the wrong change and points it out. The shopkeeper eyes her sharply: "Very accurate. Just like a Jew. Perhaps you are a little Jewess?" And Elza feels afraid and wonders if this woman sees the truth in her blue eyes.

Another memory. Elza is reading accounts of the war. She cannot help herself she tells me. An anecdote explains something to her. A woman in a camp requests a bandage for a wound. And the guard, so startled by her simplicity and directness, makes sure she gets one. That woman, Elza tells me, refused to stop acting like a human being. Jews, she concludes, made a terrible mistake.

I am walking home alone at midnight. I am raw with the pain of her death. I wonder. Is it inevitable? Everything that happened to us afterwards, to all of us, does none of it matter? Does it not matter what we do and where we live? Are there moments in history which cannot be escaped or transcended, but which act like time warps permanently trapping all those who are touched by them? And that which should have happened in 1944 in Poland and didn't, must it happen now? In 1964? In Chicago? Or can history be tricked and cheated?

These questions haunt me. Yet I persist with a will I myself do not understand. I continue reading, studying, making friends. And as the rawness of Elza's death eases and becomes familiar, as time becomes distance, I find myself more and more grounded in my present life, in my passion for words and literature. I begin to perceive the world around me. I develop perspective.

I see the rubble of this unbombed landscape, see that the city, like the rest of this alien country, is not simply a geographic place, but a time zone, an era in which I, by my very presence in it, am rooted. No one simply passes through. History keeps unfolding and demanding a response. A life obliterated around me of those I barely noticed. A life unmarked, unrecorded. A silent mass migration. Relocation. Common rubble in the streets.

I see now the present dangers, the dangers of the void, of the American hollowness in which I walk calmly day and night as I continue my life. I begin to see the incessant grinding down of lines for stamps, for jobs, for a bed to sleep in, of a death stretched imperceptibly over a lifetime. I begin to understand the ingenuity of it. The invisibility. The Holocaust without smoke.

Everything is poised. Everything is waiting for the emptiness to be filled up, for the filling-up that can never replace, that can only take over. Like time itself. Or history.

3. Brooklyn, 1971: I am almost equidistant from two continents.

I am almost equidistant from two continents. I look back towards one, then forward towards the other. The moment is approaching when I will be equidistant from both and will have to choose. Maintaining equidistance is not a choice.

By one of those minor and peculiar coincidences that permanently shape and give texture to our lives, I am born on my father's twenty-eighth birthday. Two years later, exactly three days after his thirtieth and my second birthday, he is dead in the brush factory district of the Warsaw Ghetto. His corpse is buried in a courtyard and eventually the spot blends with the rest of the rubble. The Uprising, my birth, his death—all merge and become interchangeable. That is the heritage of one continent.

In one of the classes that I teach, all the students are Black and Puerto Rican. I am the only white. Initially, the students are nervous, wondering if I will be a hard task master. I am nervous too, though I do not yet have a name for it. After a few months together, we grow accustomed to each other. I am trying to understand my role here. That is the heritage of the other continent.

And now, approaching my own thirtieth birthday, approaching the moment when I will be equidistant from the two land masses, I feel some kind of cellular breakdown in my body, a sudden surging inside me, as if flesh and muscle and bone were losing definition. Everything in me yearns to become transparent, to be everywhere, to become like the water between two vast land masses that will never touch. I desire to become salt water, to establish the connection.

I am almost equidistant from two continents.

April 17, 1955. I have been asked to light one of the six candles. I stand on the stage in the large, darkened auditorium, wait to be called, wait to accept the flame, to pass it on like a memory. I am numb with terror at the spectacle around me. I fear these people with blue numbers on their arms, people who are disfigured and scarred, who have missing limbs and uneasy walks, people whose histories repel me. Here in this auditorium, they abandon all inhibitions, they transform themselves into pure sound, the sound of irretrievable loss, of wild pain and sorrow. Then they become all flesh, wringing their hands and covering their swollen eyes and flushed faces. They call out to me and I feel myself dissolving.

When it is time for me to come forward, to light the candle for those children who were burned, who were shot, who were stomped to death, I move without feeling. And as I near the candelabra, I hear them call out the common Yiddish names: *Surele. Moyshele. Channele. Rivkele. Yankele. Shayndele. Rayzl. Benyomin. Chavele. Miriam. Chaim.* The names brush against my face, invade my ears, my mouth. I breathe them into my lungs, into my bones. And as the list continues, guided by their sounds, I cross the stage and light the sixth and final candle. It is my fourteenth birthday.

I am almost equidistant from two continents.

March, 1971. There are twenty-eight people in the class. Eighteen women, ten men. Some married. Some single. Alone. With children. With parents and grandparents. Nieces. Nephews. They are here because they have not met the minimum standards of this college. This class is their special chance to catch up. Subject and verb agreement. Sentence fragments. Pronoun reference. Vocabulary building. Paragraph organization. Topic sentence. Reading comprehension. Study skills. Discipline. All this to catch up, or as one student said to me, his eyes earnest: "I want to write so that when I go for a job they won't think I'm lazy."

I am required to take attendance. I check through the names, call them out each morning: *James. Reggie. Marie. Simone. Joy. Christine. Alvarez. Ashcroft. Basile. Colon. Corbett. White. Raphael. Dennis. Juan. Carissa. Lamont. Andrea.* Fragments of their lives fall before me. The chaos and disorganization. A mother needing help in filling out forms in English. A sick child. Hospital regulations. A brother looking for a job. Another brother in trouble. Welfare red tape. Unemployment payment restrictions. Waiting lists. Eviction. SRO. The daily grind interrupting their catching-up, and the increasing sense that with each day missed, they fall further behind.

I am almost equidistant from two continents. I look back towards one, then forward towards the other. There is a need in me to become transparent like water, to become the salt water which is their only connection.

March, 1971. Marie wants to study medicine. She concedes it's a long haul, but, as she says, "It's only time. What difference does it make?" Slightly older than the others, she lives alone with her daughter. To some of the women's horror, she refuses to have a telephone, does not like to be intruded upon. When necessary, she can always be reached through a neighbor. She rarely misses class, on a few occasions brings her daughter with her who sits serenely drawing pictures. Facing Marie, I sometimes do not know who I am and wonder how she perceives me. She seems oblivious to my discomfort. She is only focused on the class, always reworking her assignments, reading everything twice, asking endless questions to make sure she really understands. One day, at the end of the hour, when we are alone, she asks: "What are you?" I am caught off guard, know the meaning of the question, but feel the resistance in me. I break it down and answer quietly: "A Jew." She nods and in that moment two vast land masses touch.

Each continent has its legacy. The day I reach my thirtieth birthday, the age of my father's death, I am equidistant from both. And as the moment passes, everything in me becomes defined again. I am once again muscle, flesh, bone. America is not my chosen home, not even the place of my birth. Just a spot where it seemed safe to go to escape certain dangers. But safety, I discover, is only temporary. No place guarantees it to anyone forever. I have stayed because there is no other place to go. In my muscles, my flesh, my bone, I balance the heritages, the histories of two continents.

4. Cherry Plain, 1981: I have become a keeper of accounts.

There are moments when I suddenly become breathless, as if I had just tricked someone, but was afraid the ruse would be exposed and I'd be hunted again. At those moments, the myths that propel our history, that turn fiction into fact, emerge in full force in me, as I stare into the eyes of strangers or someone suddenly grown alien. And when I see their eyes become pinpoints of judgments, become cold and indifferent, or simply distanced with curiousity, at those moments I hear again the words of the Polish woman:

Very accurate. Just like a Jew. You are perhaps a little Jewess?

At moments such as these I teeter, shed the present, and like rage, like pride, like acceptance, like the refusal to deny, I call upon the ancient myths again and say:

Yes. It's true. All true. I am scrupulously accurate. I keep track of all distinctions. Between past and present. Pain and pleasure. Living and surviving. Resistance and capitulation. Will and circumstances. Between life and death. Yes. I am scrupulously accurate. I have become a keeper of accounts.

Like the patriarchs, the shabby scholars who only lived for what was written and studied it all their lives

Like the inhuman usurers and dusty pawnbrokers who were quarantined within precisely prescribed limits of every European town and who were as accurate as the magistrates that drew the boundaries of their lives and declared them diseased

Like those men of stone who insisted that the *goyim* fulfil the contracts they had signed and who responded to the tearful pleas of illness, weakness, sudden calamity and poverty, with the words: "What are these to me? You have made me a keeper of accounts. Give me my pound of flesh. It says on this piece of paper, you owe me a pound of flesh!"

Like those old, heartless, dried up merchants whose entire lives were spent in the grubby *shtetl* streets that are now but memory, whose only body softness was in their fingertips worn smooth by silver coins, whose vision that all that mattered was on pieces of paper was proven absolutely accurate, when their

złoty, francs, and marks could not buy off the written words
Żyd, Juif, Jude

Like these, my despised ancestors
I have become a keeper of accounts.

And like all the matriarchs, the wives and daughters, the sisters
and aunts, the nieces, the keepers of button shops, milliners,
seamstresses, peddlers of foul fish, of matches, of rotten apples,
laundresses, midwives, floor washers and street cleaners, who
rushed exhausted all week so that *shabes* could be observed
with fresh *challah* on the table, who argued in the common
tongue

and begged for the daughter run off to the revolution
and the daughter run off with a *shegetz*
who refused to sit *shiva* and say *kaddish* for a living child
who always begged for life
who understood the accounts but saw them differently
who knew the power of human laws, knew they always counted
no matter what the revolution or the party or the state
who knew the power of the words *Żyd, Juif, Jude*

who cried whole lifetimes for their runaway children
for the husbands immobilized by the written word
for the brother grown callous from usury
for the uncle grown indifferent from crime, from bargaining,
from chiseling, from jewing them down

Like these, my despised ancestors
I have become a keeper of accounts.

I do not shun this legacy. I claim it as mine   whenever I see
the photographs of nameless people. Standing staring off the
edge of the picture. People dressed in coats lined with fur. Or
ragged at elbows and collar. Hats cocked on one side glancing
anxiously toward the lens. A peasant cap centered and ordinary.
Hair styled in the latest fashion. Or standing ashamed a coarse
wig awkwardly fitted. The shabby clothes. Buttons missing. The
elegant stance. Diamond rings. Gold teeth. The hair being
shaved. The face of humiliation. The hand holding the child's
hand. A tree. A track. A vague building in a photograph. A fa-

cility. And then the fields of hair   the endless fields of hair
the earth growing fertile with their bodies   with their souls.

Old   rarely seen types. Gone   they say   forever. And yet I
know they can be revived again   that I can trigger them again.
That they awaken in me   for I have felt it happen   in the
sight of strangers   or someone suddenly grown alien. When-
ever I have seen the judgment   the coldness   and indiffer-
ence   the distanced curiousity.   At those moments   I
teeter   shed my present self   and all time merges   and
like rage   like pride   like acceptance   like the refusal to
deny   I answer

Yes. It is true.   I am a keeper of accounts.

Bashert

Solitary Acts

for my aunt
Gina Klepfisz (1908?-1942)

> "To garden is a solitary act."
> —Michelle Cliff

1.

And to die
as you did   with the father
confessor   standing   waiting
patiently   for your death
for your final words
and you   watching the dissolution
around you   watching his eyes
his face   listening to his Latin words
said: "What have I to confess?
I am a Jew."

It was 1942   and you wanted someone
to know   though you'd be buried
in a Christian grave   with an Aryan name.

Such will to be known   can alter history.

2.

Today   I stand alone   planning my first garden
and think of you   buried on that other continent
rescued from the Christian plot
the only flesh of your family   to lie
in a marked grave   in the Jewish cemetery
in a Warsaw   almost empty of any Jews.
That ground   I know   is but a fragment
of the past   a place apart   the surroundings
long rebuilt   into a modern city
and I know   that even now
while I stand   and try to map this season's growth
that country   cleansed of our people's blood
intones the litany of old complaints.

Gina   they hate us still.

3.

You are to me   everything
that remains   outside my grasp
everything   in this world
that is destroyed   with no one
there to rescue the fragments
to hear the words.
So much of history   seems
a gaping absence   at best a shadow
longing   for some greater
definition   which will never come
for what is burned   becomes air
and ashes   nothing more.

So I cling   to the knowledge of your
distant grave   for it alone
reminds me   prods me   to shape that shadow.

4.

I have spent a life   disentangling from influences
trying to claim   what was original   mine:
from my mother's mastery   of daily survival
so subtly interwoven   with common gestures
few recognize it   for what it is
from my father's more visibly   heroic deed
of dying   recorded in memoirs   tributes
from the deaths of grandparents   aunts   uncles
anonymous   in a heap   indistinguishable
from all the others   who died unmourned.

And now   I remember you   and face another:
Gina   in those few months   when you watched
over me   before my consciousness learned
the danger   into which I had just been born
and the label   of who I was   and while my mother
sick and weak   teetered on the edge of life
in those few months   as the meaning of the ghetto
walls   grew more defined   as you inched people
out of the *umschlagplatz*   your chest contracting
gasping   with fear   yet certain that this needed to be done
I believe   that in that short time   something
passed between us   Gina   and you imparted to me
the vision   the firm sense of self   that gave
you strength   to state your name.

5.

And who would say   that I have mourned
enough   that I have looked at the old
photographs enough   yellowed and faded
and the green ink   now a grey dullness
where Marek   placed the flowers
on the rubble   where my father's body
was buried and disappeared   and Marek's head
looking down   his profile   etched against
an empty horizon   for there was nothing left

who would say   that I have mourned
enough?

And when I asked my mother if I
could have this album   that holds it all
holds more than most have   who are
without a witness   to mark their spot in green
or whose graves have been overgrown by weeds
or forests   or bulldozed for the sake
of modern cities   or whose bodies were never
buried   but were left for speechless animals
to devour   there is no piece of earth
that does not have its nameless   who lived
and died   unnoticed   beyond the grasp of history
who die today

And when I asked my mother   if I
could have this album   and she replied
this stays here   in this apartment
until I die   I glimpsed again the urgency
to be known.

6.

There have been many plots of ground
that formed me. This town's church
its cemetery   the bare   expectant earth
of my garden   all remind me   of that
other soil   on which I grew.

The first   was the green bush and grass
behind Marek's house in Lodz. It was
after the war   and Elza   orphaned   and just recently
claimed   from the Polish stranger   stood proud
before me   and brushed her long blond hair
her haughtiness   her only power. I watched
ashamed   and awkward   my small hand trying
to hide   my bald head   shaved for reasons
I was never told. It was our first meeting.

More than two years later   in the neutral
countryside that never saw the war   in Neglinge
Moti and I   crawled flat on our stomachs
to see the miniature wild flowers   hidden
beneath the blooming lilac bush. They grew
for elves   I said   and bound him to me
with the secret   not wanting anyone else
to know. He was alert then   but only months
before   had refused to eat   was force fed
in a Stockholm hospital. When his appetite
returned   he clung to me   four years older
in a way   no one could ever understand
and I responded   as I never would again
unconsciously   selflessly   with complete
certainty.   I knew that he must live
and inched him along.

And again   a few years later   in a park   the Bronx
there was an unmowed field   near a metal fence.
My mother would bring me here   on warm summer Sundays
and spread a blanket   that would billow
over the high   resistant grass   then finally settle
and flatten with the weight of our bodies.
We brought things to read   books that warmed

with the sun   newspapers   that yellowed
as the day wore on.

These were the gardens of my childhood.

7.

Gina   I must tell you: today I
felt hopeful   as I knelt close
to the earth   and turned it
inch by inch   sifting the soil
clearing the way   for roots
of vegetables. I felt so hopeful
Gina   that with repeated years
and efforts   the monotony of daily
motion   of bending   and someday
the earth   would be uncluttered
the debris cleared.

There is   I know   no reason
for such hope   for nothing destroyed
is ever made up   or restored to us.
In the earth   are buried histories
irretrievable.   Yet what philosophy
can justify   any of our emotions?
Like the watercolors from Buchenwald—
if you can imagine! The stench
from the chimneys   just the sounds
of the place. And yet someone felt
a need to paint. And did.

So do not ask me to explain
why I draw meaning and strength
from these common gestures   why today
my hope is unwavering   solid   as if
I'd never lost it   or never would again
as if those dying   angry or stunned
at the stupidity of it   could be revived
as if their mortal wounds   could heal
as if their hunger   could be outlived
as if they were not dying   strangers
to others   strangers to themselves.

I need to hope. And do.

8.

I have been a dreamer   dreaming
of a perfect garden   of a family tree
whose branches   spread   through centuries
of an orderly cemetery   with no gravestones
missing.   Tonight   as the sun sets   and I
turn towards evening   I have no such dreams.
Like the woman   who refused to trace
the ancient constellations   upon a clear
and crowded sky   because finding the stars
recording each in its place   the faint
and the brilliant   was enough
I too   Gina   have discarded all patterns
and blueprints. This night   I want only
to sleep   a dark   rich   dreamless sleep
to shelter   in me   what is left
to strengthen myself   for what is needed.

Cherry Plain, New York
August 1982

periods of stress

herr captain
    zeyde (Yiddish) — grandfather
    bobe (Yiddish) — grandmother

death camp
    rebitsin (Yiddish) — wife of a rabbi
    rebe (Yiddish) — rabbi

The Journal of Rachel Robotnik

robotnik (Polish,m) — worker

Keeper of Accounts

IV. Inhospitable Soil

"i can't go back. . . " from "Notes of an Immigrant Daughter: Atlanta" by Melanie Kaye in *Nice Jewish Girls: A Lesbian Anthology*, ed. Evelyn Torton Beck (Watertown, Massachusetts: Persephone Press Inc., 1982).

Glimpses of the Outside

Ich habe ein kleines kind. (German) I have a small child.

Bashert

goyim (Yiddish, pl.)—Gentiles
shtetl (Yiddish)—small-town Jewish community in Eastern Europe, where Yiddish culture flourished; these towns were completely destroyed by the end of World War II
złoty, francs, marks—Polish French, German monetary units
Żyd, *Juif, Jude* (Polish, French, German)—Jew
shabes (Yiddish)—Sabbath

challah (Yiddish)—a twisted white bread eaten on the Sabbath
shegetz (Yiddish)—Gentile man (pejorative)
shiva (Yiddish)—a seven-day mourning period for the dead
kaddish (Yiddish)—a prayer for the dead

Solitary Acts

"To garden is a solitary act." from "The Garden" in *Claiming an Identity They Taught Me to Despise* by Michelle Cliff (Watertown, Massachusetts: Persephone Press Inc., 1980).

umschlagplatz (German)—the place of deportation for concentration camps

"Like the watercolors from Buchenwald—" For the extraordinary artwork produced in ghettos, concentration camps and in hiding, see the reproductions in *The Art of the Holocaust,* eds. Janet Blatter and Sybil Milton (New York: Rutledge Press, 1981).